The Power of 21 Days
Identity in Christ

Jared Stump

Cover Design by Amy Pugh
Interior Design by Battle Ground Creative

Published in Dallas, Texas, by Battle Ground Creative
Revised First Edition

Day 13: Fully Convinced is adapted from Jared's upcoming book, *Creation & Redemption: Finding Your Place in a Fallen World*, available late Summer 2015 from Battle Ground Creative.

Day 17: Desire is primarily a work of fiction. Any resemblance to actual persons, living or dead, is purely coincidental.

Day 20: Community. Special thanks to Bryan Faltynski of Rapid City, South Dakota for helping me with the Ephesians research.

ISBN-13: 978-0615974163
ISBN-10: 0615974163
RELIGION / Christian Life / Devotional

To anyone who has ever questioned whether they are fully loved, forgiven, and accepted by the Father; to those who have struggled and those who still struggle to find their place in The Story … this one's for you.

Sam,

I am so impressed by your maturity and passion for God. You are a big deal! May God bless every endeavor that you put your hands to and fulfill every dream in your heart.

CONTENTS

Read This First   1

Day 1   Casualties of a World at War   3

Day 2   Not Enough?   9

Day 3   Light and Darkness   14

Day 4   A Tale of Two Fathers   19

Day 5   The Heart   24

Day 6   Your True Self   28

Day 7   Alive and Awake   34

Day 8   Breaking the Cycle of Defeat   38

Day 9   Lies We Believe   44

Day 10   God Is Like Jesus   49

Day 11   The Father's Heart   55

Day 12   Paradigm of Scarcity   60

Day 13   Fully Convinced   65

Day 14   Be Love.   72

Day 15   Powerful and Free   77

Day 16   More than the Roles You Play   83

Day 17   Desire   88

Day 18   Overlap of the Ages   97

Day 19   The Perspective of Heaven   102

Day 20   Community   111

Day 21   Shelter from the Storm   118

Read This First

The purpose of this devotional is to serve as a series of "inciting incidents" over a 21-day period, in order to lead you into a deeper revelation of your identity in Christ. I don't expect this devotional to change your life or completely transform you in three weeks. I do, however, believe it can help begin the process, which is why I call it an inciting incident. Only Jesus can change your life, and I pray that you find Him in these pages.

It is strongly recommended that you read through this devotional in order, as the entries build upon one another. If you're like me, you probably want to bounce all over the place, or perhaps read through all 21 days in a single sitting. Don't do this. It will take you at least 20 minutes a day to read each entry and think about what you've read. This devotional is pretty in-depth, so you will get the most out of it if you read it in a more relaxed season of life, rather than when you're constantly moving at 90 MPH. (If you've been moving at this speed for quite some time, I can recommend a few books on the topic of Sabbath.)

This devotional is probably unlike any that you're ever utilized before. The readings will pry at the hidden parts of your soul. The questions will sometimes be difficult to answer. The activations may frustrate those of you who like formulas. Some days, they will include practical steps; other days, they will include an additional thought to think over. I'm not opposed to formulas, but I know they can sometimes get in the way of God speaking to the heart. If that's you, give yourself permission to think outside of the box for the next 21 days. This is about you encountering God and Him introducing you to your true self, not you achieving a "new and improved" version of yourself.

Writing this devotional has been a very freeing experience for me. Negative ways of thinking have been revealed for what they are, and I have been inspired by what the future can be. You're not alone on this journey. There are others who have gone before you, and the Father is with you always—to the very end of the age.

May your eyes be opened to see what is most true about you. May the Father reveal to you who you already are. May His love invade your heart, as every lie of the enemy is erased. May you discover your *Identity in Christ*.

Jared Stump
Frisco, Texas
February 2014

DAY 1
CASUALTIES OF A WORLD AT WAR

Do you ever find yourself asking questions like, "Where was God?"

Yeah, me too.

Last summer, I was with some friends in a grocery store in Salt Lake City, when I met a man named Mike. He had served as a greeter there for sixteen years, and he only had one arm. He had grown up in a religious system of sorts, but had gotten burned somewhere along the way.

"I don't believe that this world just happened, but I struggle to believe in the Christian God," he told me.

"Why is that?" I asked him.

"I just don't think I can trust a God who demands to be worshiped all the time. Is He really that insecure? And I don't know what to do with all of the suffering in this world. I mean, Jesus suffered for a few hours on the cross, but what about people who suffer their entire lives?"

We continued to talk to Mike for a while, and then my friend Megan asked if she could pray for him. He nodded, bowing his head. The presence of God swept through the store as people milled about around us. After she was finished praying, Megan told Mike that she would continue to pray that the Father reveals Himself to him.

He looked her square in the eyes, nodding. "Thank you. I hope He does."

I'll never forget that response. There was an intense longing and desire spilling out of his heart—mostly through his eyes. He was crying out to know his true Father.

"This world has gone terribly wrong," I told him as we were turning to go. "But God is making all things new."

"Yeah, but there's still a lot of evil in this world," he said.

"I know. But someday, there won't be."

"I'm looking forward to that day."

We exited into the parking lot. I put my arm around Megan as we walked, both of us on the verge of breaking down in tears.

When I think back on this encounter, the thing that strikes me the most is this man—who only had one arm—never once pointed to himself as an example of suffering. I think this was because he knew that suffering is not unique to him. Whether he realized it or not, he was becoming more and more aware that *we live in a world at war.*

In one way or another, we are all casualties of this war, but that does not mean we have to be victims. Though he may not be able to put words to it, Mike knows that he is a casualty of a world at war. He knows that he is not living wholeheartedly, that he is not experiencing life the way it was meant to be lived. Yet, he is not a victim.

When I meet people who have been affected by the war (which is everyone, by the way), they usually slide into one of two extremes. Either they have no idea that they are living in the midst of a war zone, or they are acutely aware of this reality, and have adopted a victim mindset as a result. Both extremes are dangerous.

You know what I love about Mike? He sees past his own problems to the larger, universal problems that everyone wrestles with. He may not be a follower of Jesus, but he is somewhat of a theologian—and he doesn't even realize it! I know plenty of people who follow Jesus, but lean toward the extreme of not realizing the world has gone terribly wrong, that we are at war. Isn't it funny to think that someone who doesn't follow Jesus can understand the brokenness of the world better than someone who does?

A theology that only heals your personal pain is far too small; we need a theology that heals the world that causes our hearts to get broken in the first place, that brings peace to the world at war and heals the wounds of her victims.

This may sound crazy, but I think we could all be a little more like Mike—open to ask questions, process new ways of viewing things, even wrestle with God. Because the moment we think we know everything, we can't learn anything.

I didn't have answers for all of Mike's questions, but now that I think about it, I do have an answer to one. Mike asked why there are some people who suffer their entire lives when Jesus only suffered on the cross for a few hours.

This is a valid question. However, it is not an accurate question. The reality is, Jesus didn't *just* suffer on the cross for a few hours. Isaiah tells us that Jesus was a man of suffering, familiar with pain.

He had no beauty of majesty to attract us to him, nothing in his appearance that we should desire him. He was despised and rejected by mankind, a man of suffering, and familiar with pain. Like one from whom people hide their faces he was despised, and we held him in low esteem. ~ Isaiah 53:2b-3

Perhaps you have been presented with some sort of fairy-tale Jesus, a man's man who looked more like Tom Cruise or Brad Pitt than the homeless man on the street corner. That isn't what Jesus was really like. In reality, He was average at best and ugly at worst. And if He was *despised* and *held in low esteem,* chances are He was probably more of the latter.

The question that Mike was asking may not have been true, but it was certainly valid—not just because it was a good thought to ponder, but because it was something that was important to Mike. In the same way, the things that are important to us, the things we wrestle with, the questions we ask, are valid because we are valuable to God.

I could have opened my Bible to Isaiah 53 and explained to Mike why he was wrong, but that was not what he needed. He needed someone to value him, to listen to what he had to say, to struggle with him. By entering into his story, rather than deflecting his questions with apologetic answers, we were showing him the heart of the Father.

Jesus became human ... the type of human no one would want to be—despised and rejected by men. ~ Brian Zahnd

Questions

1) Have you ever realized (before reading this devotional) that you live in a world at war?

2) How has living in a world at war affected you?

3) Can you relate to any of the questions that Mike was wrestling with?

Activation

As followers of Jesus, we sometimes live with the mentality that we have to have all the answers, that there can't be any room for doubts in our minds. This goes hand-in-hand with the mentality that Christias have to be happy all of the time, as if our faith requires one to empty their brain and put on a giant happy face. That's not following Jesus; that's being a phony.

As you begin this 21-day journey, I invite you to open up your mind and heart to everything God wants to speak to you. Leave all of your preconceived notions behind. Check your religious baggage at the door. This is a journey where all you need is yourself and God.

DAY 2
NOT ENOUGH?

Do you remember the first time you discovered that the world is broken?

I remember when my cousin was born, while I was still in high school. In the days and weeks after she came home from the hospital, I would hold her in my arms for hours, and just stare at her as she slept. I couldn't quite pinpoint what it was, but she just seemed so pure, so innocent, so ... unaffected.

As she grew up, I would look on as she lived life in childlike wonder, and I would think back to when I used to be like that. We all start out this way, but it's usually not long before we become casualties of a world at war.

I remember one day when she was upset because her hair "wasn't pretty enough." I was immediately taken aback. I began to think back to the beginning of The Story, when God was walking in the garden, looking for His kids after their first encounter with a broken world—or rather, when they first broke the world.

Then the man and his wife heard the sound of the Lord God as he was walking in the garden in the cool of the day, and they hid from the Lord God among the trees of the garden. But the Lord God called to the man, "Where are you?"

He answered, "I heard you in the garden, and I was afraid because I was naked; so I hid."

And he said, "Who told you that you were naked? Have you eaten from the tree that I commanded you not to eat from?"

~ *Genesis 3:8-11*

When we read the rest of the story in Genesis, we see that there were two trees in the garden: the Tree of the Knowledge of Good and Evil and the Tree of Life. Adam and Eve were told not to eat from the former, but they could partake freely of the latter. Have you ever wondered why this was the case?

Simply put, God designed mankind to draw their source of life from Him alone. He never intended for us to live in a world where the opposing forces of good and evil are at play; He designed us to live in a world where all we know is *life*. This word has become quite generic in our culture, but I reckon it to *shalom*, the Hebrew word for *peace*, which means *wholeness, nothing broken or missing.*

God also created us with free will. Adam and Eve were not robots. God gave them one simple command, "Don't eat from this tree. If you do, you will no longer be able to live life in the way that you were created to."

When Adam and Eve disobeyed God, they didn't just commit a small, personal sin. Rather, they created an entire system of sin. Our actions are always more far-reaching than we realize. Adam and Eve didn't just bring brokenness into the human race, they brought brokenness into the world itself. They started the war that we are still fighting today.

Who told you that you were naked?

Adam and Eve were naked before, and it wasn't like they were oblivious to that, there just wasn't any shame in it. But when they brought sin into the world, shame came with it.

Shame can be very powerful. It's what caused Adam and Eve to hide from a God who already knew them fully and loved them completely—even in their brokenness. When their eyes were opened to the knowledge of good and evil, they realized that they were not enough, that they were not qualified to partake of the life that God offered, so they hid.

We aren't much different from Adam and Eve. When we feel that we are not enough, we tend to hide from God. This only furthers the problem, because God is the only one who can validate us with the reality that, in Him, we *are* enough. He comes to us, just as He did Adam and Eve, in all of the places where we try to hide. When He finds us,

He doesn't condemn us, but this doesn't mean He doesn't talk to us about what caused us to hide in the first place.

Who told you that your failure isn't fixable?

Who told you that you aren't worthy of love?

It isn't just our own brokenness that causes us to hide from God; the brokenness of the world itself sends us into hiding. Sometimes it's what we've done wrong that tells us that we are not enough, but other times, it's what has been done to us, or perhaps what has been said to us.

Who told you that your hair wasn't pretty enough?

Who told you that you don't have what it takes?

More than our own brokenness, life itself has a way of telling us that we are not enough, which is why we need God to tell us that we *are*. While it's good to hear that we are beautiful, talented, faithful, and all of those things, what we need most is for God to tell us that we are *enough*.

But by the grace of God I am what I am ... ~ 1 Corinthians 15:10

Questions

1) In what ways do you feel that you are not enough?
2) Are there any areas of your life that are broken?
3) Has any of this caused you to hide from God?

Activation

Be still. Slow down. Let God speak. Let His presence invade the secret places of your heart.

As you identify areas of your life where you have been hiding from God, invite Him into those areas. This doesn't have to be complex; just ask Him to come into that part of your life and fill it with everything that He is. Brokenness doesn't stand a chance against the God who knows you better than you know yourself, yet still tells you that you are His and that you are enough.

DAY 3
LIGHT AND DARKNESS

When we look at our lives, we often see a conflict between light and darkness. As we discussed yesterday, our darkness (or brokenness) often causes us to hide from God in shame—because we're Christians, and we think Christians are supposed to have all of their junk taken care of immediately after conversion, so when we read verses like *what fellowship can light have with darkness?* (2 Corinthians 6:14), we feel even more shame.

It almost seems counterproductive to talk about sin in a discussion about identity in Christ, because sin no longer has the power to define those who are in Christ. We are not the sins we commit; our sin is not what is most true about us. Still, it is important that we discuss this, as it will give us clues to what is going on inside of us.

Most of us default to describing sin as *bad stuff we should avoid.* There is some truth to that, but ultimately, that definition of sin is incomplete. Sin is far more reaching than just our actions.

Sin is a *condition* before it ever becomes a *behavior.* This means that what we think is a behavior problem is really just the fruit of something much deeper, something that is usually wrapped up in our identity.

I would define sin as *the absence of God,* and darkness as *the absence of life.*

When we define sin as the absence of God, we are describing a condition, not a behavior. God is absent from the hearts of those who are not in Christ; therefore, they don't have any choice but to follow their sin nature. Their behavior flows out of their condition. But as we discussed yesterday, there can be areas of our lives where we hide from God. Areas where God is absent, even though we are in Christ. And if God is the source of life, than when He is absent, life is absent. In this we see how sin and darkness go hand-in-hand.

Darkness always has an agenda: *to prevent us from connecting to God and becoming fully human.* Before Adam and Eve fell, they didn't have to worry about *avoiding bad stuff.* They were connected to God, full of life and light. They were *fully human.*

Finding our identity in Christ in this present age is about retracing humanity's steps back to the garden in order to recover the life we've lost. It's about discovering why we do the things that make us less than human, and inviting God to shine His light on those places of our lives. In other words, when we find our identity in Christ, we are able to fully connect to God and thus become fully human. This does not happen overnight. Becoming who you already are is a lifelong process. But when God looks at you, He doesn't see the conflict between light and darkness—He sees who you already are! That's right: you are *already* righteous, because of the blood of Jesus. In God's eyes, you're already at the finish line. But in your present reality, you're still in the process. This isn't a license to sin, but a tension you must wrestle with. (Why would you want to make yourself less than human, which is what sin does?)

Many Christians have been taught that their sin separates them from God. An obscure verse from Isaiah is often quoted to provide evidence for this theory. And it is true that sin separates those who are not in Christ from God, because sin itself is the absence of God.

But we are in Christ; our lives are hidden in Him (Colossians 3:3), so in order for our sin to separate us from God, God would have to stop looking at us through the blood of Jesus. Nothing outside of us can separate us from God's love (Romans 8:38-39) or destroy our position in Christ—not even our sin. The *only* thing that can separate us is ... us.

Even though we are in Christ, we can still live our lives as if He is absent. When we do this, darkness sets in. We become less than human. And the crazy thing is, we can compartmentalize our lives to where God is present in one area and absent from another. (We do this all the time.) Yet, it is not our sin that separates us from God, but our perception of our sin. When we focus on our light, we move toward the light. When we focus on our darkness, we move toward the darkness. When we fix our eyes on Jesus, we realize that what He started in us when He saved us, He will finish in us when we see Him face-to-face (Hebrews 12:2). When we fix our eyes on Jesus, we will move toward the light naturally, and we will realize that it is Jesus doing His work inside of us, rather than our own efforts getting us to Him.

The goal of the Christian life is not to sin less frequently (though that is a natural by-product). Jesus did not come to make bad people behave; He came to restore what was lost in the garden, to show us the way back to life and help us become fully human—fully ourselves.

You, LORD, are my lamp; the LORD turns my darkness into light. ~ 2 Samuel 22:29

God has delivered me from going down to the pit, and I shall live to enjoy the light of life. ~ Job 33:28

Questions

1) How has this discussion changed the way you think about sin?

2) How is your perception of your sin keeping you from coming to God?

Activation

When we find ourselves in darkness, the shame that comes with it often keeps us from opening up that part of us to God, which is what we need the most. God is not afraid of our darkness, and He wants us to be raw and real with Him, no matter how messy that may be.

Today, try to live completely honest with God. Talk to Him about the things you would be terrified to mention in church. Get a little messy—He can handle it. He already knows you completely and loves you perfectly, so why wouldn't you want to be honest with Him?

At the end of the day, take some time to reflect. Does your relationship with God feel different? Do you feel closer to Him?

Throughout this 21-day discussion (and for the rest of your life), commit to live this way.

DAY 4
A TALE OF TWO FATHERS

Yesterday, we discussed the tension between light and darkness that often plays out inside of us. It reminds us that we live in a world that has gone horribly wrong, and while God is restoring the life we've lost, we're not there yet. This tension is a normal part of the Christian life. That doesn't mean that it is what God has for you, but it is often reality, and I think it is important for you to know that you are not the only one wrestling with this.

In its simplest form, the Gospel is the story of a Father who is on a mission to get His kids back. When Adam and Eve chose to walk away from God, they did so on behalf of the entire human race, so that we are born separated from our True Father. The Gospel is not a story of how we wandered away from home, but a story of how we were born away from home, surrounded by darkness, so that we could not find our way home. We begin as orphans, but a loving Father is ready and waiting to adopt us—and He's not just waiting for us, He's actually *looking* for us. He has to find us, because we are in darkness. Without His light, we can't find our way to Him.

1 John 1:5 tells us that God is light, and because of this, there is no darkness in Him. Genesis 1:26 says that God made us in His image. In other words, He deposited everything that He is inside of us. So if God is light, and we are made in His image, where did our darkness come from? If we didn't get that from God, we must have gotten it from someone else.

God is the True Father of the entire human race, and He is a good Father. But there is another father out there—a fraud, a counterfeit, a phony, *the bad father*—whose name is satan. The True Father is King over the light, while the bad father is king over the darkness.

The light shines in the darkness, and the darkness has not overcome it. ~ *John 1:5*

The two fathers are at war with one another, but the game has already been fixed. satan knows that the True Father has already defeated him; yet, he continues to fight.

Why fight if the contest has already been decided? More importantly, what are they even fighting for?

They are fighting for you and for me—for our hearts.

The True Father wants your heart because He treasures and values it, but the bad father is only after your heart because he doesn't want the True Father to have it. He doesn't value you; he just wants to keep the One who does from being reunited with you. You were born under the rule of the bad father, but your True Father has set out to find you and bring you home—to the place where you truly belong.

When our True Father brings us home, it's sometimes hard to unlearn the ways of the bad father, because that's all we've ever known. But our True Father is patient with us as we learn His ways, and discard the ways of the bad father. The light in us came from our True Father, while the darkness came from our bad father. So why isn't darkness gone once the bad father is out of the picture?

When our True Father finds us and rescues us from the bad father, the bad father doesn't shrink back in defeat. If anything, he goes even more on the offensive. The bad father is still lurking in the shadows when we get out of bed each morning. This shouldn't scare us, because we know that our True Father has already won and we are secure in Him, but we must also be aware that the bad father will try to win us back. He has no power to forcefully *take* us back, but he is a master of deception, and he will try to get us to come back *on our own.*

The bad father doesn't have very many tricks up his sleeve. In fact, all he really does is twist and distort things that are true. He spins a web of lies in our direction, trying to erode our beliefs about who God is and who we are. The tricky thing is, his lies are often partially true. He tries to convince us that our darkness, rather than our light, is what is most true about us. If he can accomplish this, he can make us believe that he is our true father again, that we have returned to the world we were born into, the world in which we were previously enslaved.

You're sons of Light, daughters of Day. We live under wide open skies and know where we stand. ~ 1 Thessalonians 5:5, MSG

Questions

1) What are some of the ways of the bad father that you've been struggling to unlearn?

2) What are some of the ways of your True Father that you can begin walking in?

Activation

This is a passage that talks about your True Father. Read it slowly, perhaps even out loud. When you see the phrase *the flesh*, think of it as the ways of the bad father.

Therefore, brothers and sisters, we have an obligation—but it is not to the flesh, to live according to it. For if you live according to the flesh, you will die; but if by the Spirit you put to death the misdeeds of the body, you will live. For those who are led by the Spirit of God are the children of God. The Spirit you received does not make you slaves, so that you live in fear again; rather, the Spirit you received brought about your adoption to sonship. And by him we cry, "Abba, Father." The Spirit himself testifies with our spirit that we are God's children. ~ Romans 8:12-16

I like how verse 12 says that we are not obligated to live according to the ways of the bad father anymore. Paul (the author of Romans) goes on to say that the ways of the bad father will destroy us, but the ways of our True Father will give us life.

So how do we get rid of the ways of the bad father?

By the Spirit.

... but if by the Spirit you put to death the misdeeds of the body (the ways of the bad father), you will live.

This may sound a bit intense, even frightening to some. But if this idea puts fear in your heart, know that it is the bad father lying to you. Paul goes on to say in verse 15 that the Spirit does not make us slaves to fear *again*. This word is key, because it tells us that when we were under the rule of the bad father, we were slaves to fear. But this is not the case with our True Father, who has adopted us as sons and placed the Holy Spirit within us to testify of that reality.

Ask the Father to reveal to you on a deeper level that you are His child, and firmly root that truth in your heart.

DAY 5
THE HEART

You can't trust yourself. Your heart will lie to you.

If you're like me, you've heard these phrases a time or two hundred, likely from well-meaning Christians. This line of thought is taken from a verse in Jeremiah that describes the heart as *deceitful above all things* and *beyond cure*. But then there are other verses, such as Proverbs 4:23, which tells us, *Above all else, guard your heart, for everything you do flows from it.*

So which is it? Is your heart deceitful and beyond cure, or the headwaters from which everything you do flows?

Yes.

Jeremiah is describing our condition before Christ, when our hearts *were* bad. And if you have a bad heart, everything you do will flow from that. Jesus confirmed this when he said that a bad tree bears bad fruit, and cannot bear good fruit (Matthew 7:17-18).

Jeremiah got it right in describing what he saw around him, but his words are not the final words. Ezekiel comes on the scene shortly thereafter, and declares, *I will give you a new heart and put a new spirit in you; I will remove from you your heart of stone and give you a heart of flesh* (Ezekiel 36:26).

Ezekiel saw what was around him, but he also saw what was to come. He didn't just see the problem, he saw the remedy. In today's terms, we refer to this as *salvation.*

Salvation is not about making a commitment to attend church or to become a better person. It's about *transformation.* When this takes place, God gives you a new heart with new desires—a heart that wants to love Him, that doesn't want to go the way of the bad father anymore. If you try to go the way of your True Father without having your heart transformed, you'll only end up tired and frustrated. As Jesus said, if you make the tree good (by transforming the heart), the fruit will be good as well (Matthew 12:33)

In one of his letters, the Apostle Paul prayed that Jesus would dwell in the people's hearts through faith (Ephesians 3:17). If their hearts were still *beyond cure,* it would not be possible for Jesus to dwell in them; their hearts had to be made new.

The heart is central. Don't bury it. Don't try to suppress it out of fear that it will deceive you. You can trust the heart that Jesus gave you. You can trust *yourself,* because He has made you new.

But I don't feel new. I don't feel that my heart is good.

25

Welcome to the struggle. Fortunately, God is bigger than how we feel. His truth is more powerful than any lie we've been convinced is true.

In 1 John 3, we are urged not to let our love be mere talk, but to actually love others. John goes on to say this is how we know we are God's children. And then, in verse 20, he says, *If our hearts condemn us, we know that God is greater than our hearts ...*

So even if you don't *feel* that your heart is good, if you have a relationship with Jesus, it is!

Sometimes, the transformation of your heart is an event that you can point back to, but other times, it's a process. There may not be a specific event you can reference, but you can say without a doubt that Jesus has changed everything, and that has made all the difference.

Your heart is good. Embrace it, just as you embrace the One who created it.

The story of your life is the story of a long and brutal assault on your heart by the one who knows what you could be and fears it.

~ John Eldredge

Questions

1) Have you ever been told that you can't trust your heart? How did this affect the way that you lived?

2) Do you find it easy to trust yourself, or are you most often suspicious of yourself?

3) What is your heart saying to you right now?

Activation

Begin listening to your heart. Don't worry about whether the content is good or bad, just listen. As you train yourself to do this, it will begin to pull back the layers that have kept your heart hidden. God wants your heart to be open, so that He can speak straight from His heart to yours. Ask Him to heal any destructive ways of thinking that have convinced you that your heart cannot be trusted.

DAY 6
YOUR TRUE SELF

Who are you?

If I were to ask you this simple question, you probably wouldn't have a hard time answering it. But what if I told you that your answer couldn't include your occupation, family name, relational connections, or even what you're most passionate about?

Many of us have no idea who we really are. Because we are not in touch with our true selves, we live out of our false selves by default. But what is a false self? And what is a true self?

Your true self is who you were created to be, the part of you that is in the image of God. Your false self, on the other hand, is the part of you that you most often interact with, the part of you that is covering up who you really are.

Brian Zahnd, a pastor who I have heard teach on this topic, says that your true self is calm, content, wise, and unafraid. But the human story is a story of how we often live agitated, graspy, foolish, and afraid—the exact opposite of our true selves.

These characteristics of your true self are who God originally designed you—and all of humanity—to be. But because you were born into a world at war, your true self has become hidden, so that it is now nearly impossible to see. Not only has your true self been hidden, a facade has been erected in order to prevent you from finding it. This facade is your false self.

When I was younger, I played baseball on a somewhat regular basis. I wasn't very good at it, but I played anyway. I was a devoted fan of the local minor league team. I memorized the major league rosters. My room was full of trinkets and memorabilia. My family would visit baseball stadiums on our vacations, even when there wasn't a game taking place. I would watch nearly every Houston Astros game on TV.

But now, things have changed. I rarely play baseball. My trinkets fill several boxes in a closet. I have no clue who plays for what team. On family vacations, I prefer to visit churches whose pastors I podcast, even when there isn't a service taking place. And it is even impossible for me to sit through Game 7 of the World Series. Instead of baseball, I prefer to read a good book or sit in a coffee house and take in the world around me.

Looking back, I don't even see how I liked sports at all. And when I really dig deep, I can see that perhaps the reason why I gave so much of myself to sports was because that's what I was *supposed to do*. No one ever told me that it was alright to be a boy and have no interest in sports; in fact, quite a few people told me the exact opposite.

Growing up, I didn't hate sports, but I would only play them in the backyard with friends from the neighborhood. Because I wasn't very good, the idea of being on a team scared me. I was afraid of being exposed for who I really was: a boy who wasn't good at sports.

But what if that wasn't who I really was?

I also loved books growing up. One of my favorite places to go was the library. But when my mom told people how much I loved books, I would get embarrassed, as if I had been told that this wasn't who I was supposed to be. Perhaps I had, or perhaps it was just in my subconscious. Regardless, the feeling was there.

The role of a baseball fan was not part of my true self, it was just a role I began to play somewhere along the line. And there was never really a point where I consciously decided I didn't like baseball anymore. Instead, I would say that I became more interested in books and writing, followed by theology and the Kingdom of God. At the risk of sounding overly spiritual, it was when I became fascinated with the Kingdom that my love of baseball began to fade, to the point where it now no longer exists.

When I reflect on this, I can see that my true self was there all along, just not in the form it's in now. Growing up, I begged my parents to let me skip church to watch baseball games. Now, they can't force me to sit through a game, but I have been known to attend anywhere from two to six hours of church services on any given Sunday.

Back when I thought church was boring, my true self was there, but in the form of my love for books. Not that loving books was my true self, but it was a signpost pointing to the person I would later become as I began to find my true self.

I don't tell you this story to try to convert you from baseball games to church attendance, but because it paints a perfect picture of what it looks like to shed your false self so that your true self can emerge.

The way to tear down the facade of your false self is not to consider how to do it. What I mean by that is, you won't break through your false self by making "breaking through your false self" your goal. But when you begin to explore what is really in your heart, when you give yourself permission to set aside the roles you have been playing for your entire life, when you allow your true self to rise to the surface—that is when the facade of your false self begins to crumble.

You are more than the roles you play, regardless of whether you have chosen them or they have been handed to you. There is more out there than everything you have ever known. Start the search; in time, you will find your true self. Perhaps you will even find that your true self is the life you are living right now.

I long to see a generation find out who they really are.
~ Jared Stump, 2011

Questions

1) Is anything stirring in your heart right now? Take note of it; it is likely a clue pointing you to your true self.

2) Can you identify the false self that you have been hiding behind?

3) If you could do one big thing that would impact history, what would it be? Why do you think you are drawn to this thing?

Activation

Today, give yourself permission to dream! Let your mind run wild as you imagine what your life would look like if you discovered your true self. Don't think about your dream job, where you want to live, or who you want to marry. This is about *you*. Because if you don't own your own story, someone else will, and that someone else may be the bad father.

Your True Father doesn't own your story for you. He doesn't seek to control you. Rather, He empowers you to control yourself, to own your own story. (In church talk, we call this *self-control*.) When we see Him face-to-face, we will give an account for our lives (2 Corinthians 5:10). How terrible it would be to have nothing to say, because you never owned your own story.

This is the permission slip you have been waiting for. Start dreaming. Start living. Own your story. Take God along for the journey. Your faith is not about trying to follow God's footsteps, but walking with Him, hand-in-hand. He will show you the way. You might hear a voice, but it is more likely that you will hear your heart. Your heart is good. Your True Father put those desires there. Don't be afraid to follow them. And if you fail, relax. We all fail. Every failure is fixable, except a life that was never lived.

DAY 7
ALIVE AND AWAKE

The goal of this devotional is to help you wake up to who you really are, to your identity in Christ. Not that my words alone can accomplish this, but I hope to at least point you in the right direction—to the very source of life itself, your True Father.

So, I ask you, are you awake?

A few of my paradigms are currently being shattered by the John Eldredge book *Waking the Dead.* At one point, he states that *we are only a shadow of who we were meant to be.* I like to think that I am awake, but perhaps I am just beginning to wake up, and my eyes are just starting to adjust to the light.

Looking back, I see the version of myself that was alive, but not awake—my false self. I lived from that place for much of my life, and in some ways I feel as though I have just been introduced to my true self; it still feels like an acquaintance, rather than a close friend.

Unfortunately, this is how many of us live. As we brush up against a broken world, as we're confronted with our flaws and failures, as we wrestle with our light and darkness, as we seek to know our True Father and unlearn the ways of the bad father—our hearts often become buried in the process.

Above all else, guard your heart, for everything you do flows from it. ~ Proverbs 4:23

If it is true that everything we do flows from our hearts, and we happen to be living out of our false selves, rather than our true selves, then I think it is fair to say that it is because our hearts have been buried by the events of life, or perhaps misplaced entirely.

Even after God has replaced our bad hearts with good hearts, we can still bury our hearts and live out of our false selves. The work that God does is finished in a moment, but it can take us our entire lives to put aside our false selves and become fully acquainted with our true selves.

If you study theology, you likely understand that the work God does when He saves us has a *now, but not yet* aspect to it. What I mean by this is, the reality that God has given us a good heart is *now*—it has already been done. But it is *not yet* in the sense that our minds are often still programmed to the ways of our bad hearts and false selves, to the ways of the bad father.

I think one of the bad father's greatest tricks is to convince us that our hearts can't be trusted and must therefore be suppressed. If he cannot get between us and our True Father, the next best thing is to shut down the thing that *everything we do flows from*. We suppress and bury our hearts, in a way that is not unlike putting a living person in a casket and burying them in the earth. If you bury the thing that everything you do flows from, how can you live?

When we do this, we will never achieve the results we desire, because the real issue is not that our hearts need to be suppressed, but that our minds need to renewed. I know that "renewing your mind" is a fancy Bible term, so think of it as becoming acquainted with your true self, which includes learning what your True Father says about you.

Being *alive* is about having your bad heart replaced with a good heart, a work that is done by your True Father. Because before He came into our lives, we were spiritually dead. As Ephesians 2:5 tells us, He made us alive when we were dead in our sins.

Becoming *awake* is about putting off your false self, so that your true self can emerge. It's a process, so don't be hard on yourself if you don't figure it all out overnight. At the beginning of this entry, I asked if you are awake. And if I were to ask that question to myself, I'm not sure that I would know the answer, because I too am still in the process.

I want to dream again and understand what is going on inside of me.

~ Paige DeHart

Questions

1) Are you awake? Why or why not?

2) What do you think is keeping you from being awake?

3) How have you buried your heart to protect it from a world at war?

Activation

Read Ephesians 1.

This section of Scripture talks about who you are because of what your True Father has done. In order to become acquainted with your true self, it's crucial that you hear what God says about you—not just with your ears, but with your heart.

According to Ephesians 1, you are chosen, adopted, and redeemed—and that is just the beginning!

DAY 8
BREAKING THE CYCLE OF DEFEAT

Have you ever failed at anything?

Of course you have. We all fail at things throughout the course of our lives. In fact, Thomas Edison—one of the greatest inventors of our day—failed thousands of times while trying to invent the light bulb. When asked to comment about his failure, Edison replied, "I have not failed; I just found 10,000 ways that don't work."

Edison had the determination to keep moving forward, even in the face of repeated failure. For me, all it takes is one or two failed attempts before I'm ready to take myself out of the game. In fact, there are many things I'm terrified to even attempt, because I've failed at something similar in the past. Why is it that failure holds us back?

What if it's not failure that holds us back at all, but the shame that comes with it? Failure says that something doesn't work, but shame takes it a step further and says that it didn't work because of *you*. Failure is an event; shame is the meaning we associate with the event, directing it back at ourselves. Failure says, "I've made a mistake." Shame says, "I am a mistake."

Failure can happen without shame, but shame cannot happen without failure. An event doesn't always bring shame, but shame always happens from an event. Sometimes it's big, sometimes it's small, sometimes you don't even have a clue what it is, but the shame is arising from something. Sometimes it's not just one event, but a series of events. You may not feel shame when you fail at something once, but what if you continue to fail repeatedly?

Shame keeps us in the shadows, hiding from risk. Sometimes, shame is so intense that you don't want to be seen at all. Shame can actually convince people that others can merely glance at them and instantly see what a failure they are. So they run. They hide. And they certainly never risk again.

What is it that causes this hiding? Is it fear? The simple answer is *yes,* but it's a bit more complex than that. Fear alone doesn't usually hold us back. Fear is actually a normal part of life. You probably felt fear when you attempted the thing you failed at, but you went for it anyway. Then, your fear was probably primarily a fear of the unknown, but when you've failed a time or two and perhaps felt shame, you have something specific to be afraid of. When you've asked two girls to the prom and they've both responded with an aggressive *no,* you're not afraid of what you *don't* know; you're afraid of what you *do* know. You're afraid of repeating the cycle all over again. More specifically, you're afraid of rejection. Often, it's this fear of rejection that draws us into the same experiences over and over, into a cycle of defeat.

It works like this: An event occurs. Failure happens. Shame sets in. When you're given the opportunity to try again, your mind starts racing. You begin to replay the events, relive the feelings of shame. Suddenly, you find yourself terrified of failure, because you know how it feels, and you're afraid of being rejected if you fail again. This fear of rejection causes you to change the way you act and relate to others. You begin to live out of your false self, while you keep your true self locked away. You hide who you are so that you won't get hurt again.

Whether this fear of rejection is real or perceived doesn't matter, because either way it has the power to change the way you live. And ironically, it's the very things that you do to avoid rejection that cause you to experience the painful feeling all over again. People who know the real version of you find it uncomfortable to interact with the false version of you. They wonder who you've become, why you're different, but they rarely connect the dots. Sometimes, they stick with you. Other times, because they feel as though they don't know you at all, they reject you.

And on goes the cycle. Event. Failure. Shame. Fear of Rejection. Rejection. Isn't it funny how we're drawn time and time again to the experiences we fear the most? This is the cycle of defeat, and it's a vicious one.

We spend a lot more time thinking about our failures than God does. Quit memorizing who you used to be. ~ Bob Goff

Questions

1) Can you identify this cycle at work in your life?

2) Do you view your failures as primarily positive or negative?

3) Can you sense any feelings of shame that are preventing you from connecting to God or people around you?

4) What are you most afraid of today? Why?

Activation

The cycle of defeat is quite prevalent in the lives of many people. It's also possible to be defeated in one area of your life while you appear to be living victoriously on all other counts. So if you can see the cycle at work in your life, know that you're not alone. Relax. You don't have to stay there. You weren't created to live this way. God wants you to be free, and only He can set you free. If you begin striving to free yourself, you'll only continue the cycle.

When we try to free ourselves, we often work at the level of the *event*. But this does not properly address the problem, because the event itself is NOT the problem. Events happen, and when we strive to control what happens to us, we only end up repeating the cycle. The problem is not the event itself, but the meaning you assign to it.

The next stage of the cycle is *failure*. When negative events happen, if you allow the failure to define you, you'll move on to the feelings of *shame*. But if you look at the failure in a positive sense, if you look at it in terms of what you learned and how you grew as a person, you can stop the cycle before it starts.

I just found 10,000 ways that don't work.

This is what it looks like to view your failure in a positive sense. You don't have to put on a fake happy face or pretend that the failure never happened. You are simply refusing to magnify the worst part of your failure so that it cannot lie to you about your identity.

Events happen. Failure happens. But the cycle can stop there. You don't have to live in shame. You don't have to live in fear. You were created to be free. And you can be free—right now—even if you've found 10,000 ways that don't work.

Begin the practice of looking at failure in a new light. Seek to learn, to understand, to grow. Look for the positive, even if you have to dig for it. And by all means, keep moving forward!

Shame is removed through love. If shame is holding you back, ask God to reveal (and continue to reveal) His perfect love to you. As you learn to receive His love, you'll find it replacing those feelings of shame that have held your heart hostage, perhaps for a very long time.

DAY 9
LIES WE BELIEVE

As we've already discussed, once we find our way home to our True Father, the bad father doesn't just leave us alone. One of his primary strategies for ruining our lives has to do with telling us lies, which are often mixed with just enough truth that we believe them.

Last summer, I was feeling the barrage of these lies at a higher level than normal, and I was growing tired of it. I had heard Jon Acuff talk about how when he sits down at his desk to work, he keeps a notepad nearby, so he can write down his fears as they surface and continue working. I decided to do something similar, but instead of writing down my fears, I would write down the lies I was hearing. I would follow that by writing down the antidote: the truth. Sometimes I would pause and ask God to show me the truth; other times, I would just know it the minute I wrote down the lie.

At first, I wrote down lies almost every day, sometimes multiple times a day. But an interesting thing began to happen as the months progressed: I wrote down less and less lies. After a few months, I was only writing down two or three lies each month. As I write this, it's been about three weeks since I recorded a lie.

I have found that recording the lies by themselves is powerful. Because when you allow them to run wild in your head, it's easy to convince yourself that they're coming from you—or worse, God. If you allow them to remain there unchecked, you might come to believe them over time, even if you don't at first. But when you write them down, it calls them out as what they are: lies. Identifying lies is powerful, but when you write down the truth as well, it takes it to a whole new level.

While I have noticed that the overall amount of lies I hear has decreased significantly, when I do identify a lie these days, it's typically much more complex and/or sneaky than before. I've also noticed that many of the early lies carried the same theme, but now that I've identified enough of them, the pattern of lies has changed. I guess the bad father has realized that those particular strategies won't work anymore, and has moved on to others.

LIE: You are a burden to people. (Because I asked someone for help with something.)
TRUTH: You aren't a burden, you just know how to ask for help, just like you know how to give it.

LIE: You are easily angered.

TRUTH: You are slow to anger. You are patient. You are loving. You have the mind of Christ.

I recorded both of these lies/truths on the same day. In both situations, I asked God to show me the truth after I had identified the lie. In the second situation, these four phrases (all of which are in Scripture) came to me. In the first, God spoke something relevant to my life that isn't recorded in Scripture (I wasn't around back then). I think it's pretty cool that God speaks to us in both ways: through Scripture, as well as on a personal, one-on-one, heart-to-heart level. Here's another example of what that looks like:

LIE: No one cares about what you have to say. You're only valuable when you're being funny.

TRUTH: I see you. I love your story. I love everything about you.

CONTEXT: I can be a very silly person, but also a very serious person as well. (Many people only see one of these two sides of me.) I have a bit of a reputation for filming videos at church events where I ambush people, stick my iPhone in their face, ask them a completely random question, and capture their off-the-cuff response. This is pure fun, and I enjoy making people laugh when I post the videos. But in one video, I added a serious slant. After the fun and games, I shared a very personal testimony. When I posted the video, everyone commented on how funny I was, but not a single person commented on my moment of vulnerability. I know this may seem shallow, but that really got to me—and that's when the lie came in.

In that moment, God came and broke through all the lies. And you know what happened after that? A few people commented and said that my testimony was one of their favorite parts! So why couldn't that have happened before? I suppose it could have, but I think God knew that I needed to hear it from Him more than I needed to hear it from anyone else. Their words only confirmed what He already said was true about me.

Humans are the only creatures capable of lying to themselves and believing their own lie. ~ Bob Hamp

Questions

1) Just from reading this, are any lies that you might believe coming to your mind?

2) Does the idea of hearing God speak seem easy or intimidating to you?

Activation

Ask your True Father to show you if you have believed any lies about who He is or who you are. This may require sitting in silence for an extended period of time while things begin to stir in your mind. Remember, lies are often rooted in partial truth—they may be true to a certain extent, but they are not *truth*.

Example: *That's so cool that George was able to lead that stranger to Jesus. I would be afraid to do something like that.*

Do you see the lie there? This person is clearly believing a lie about their abilities, but also God's willingness to operate through them. Romans 2:11 tells us that God does not play favorites. Do you see how believing this lie could stop this person from doing the same thing that George did?

Remember, hearing God doesn't have to be spooky or intimidating. It may seem a bit mystical, but the idea that we believe in a God we can't see and worship Him is already a very mystical idea in itself. I've heard an audible voice once (and have a witness who can confirm it), but most of the time, it's just a thought that pops into my head that aligns with the heart of God as revealed in Scripture.

Hearing from God is a normal part of the Christian life. In fact, you may have been hearing Him for a while now, but thought it was just a distraction from your quiet time.

DAY 10
GOD IS LIKE JESUS

When many people think of the Trinity, they think of God as *the mean one,* Jesus as *the nice one,* and the Holy Spirit as *the weird one.* They view the God of the Old Testament as angry, Jesus in the New Testament as kind and compassionate, and the Holy Spirit as the one that makes people crazy. While the members of the Trinity are distinct and carry out different roles, they do not have contradictory personalities.

The story of the Bible is not a story of a mean God who suddenly became nice halfway through. It's a story of a God who is deeply emotional and compassionate, who relentlessly loves and pursues His people, who experiences heartbreak and pain when they walk away from Him. If you've ever had someone close to you walk out of your life, you know exactly how this feels.

God sent Jesus into the world because *He* loved the world. Saving the world through Jesus was God's idea from the moment things went wrong; it wasn't something that Jesus came up with on His own and God reluctantly agreed to. Jesus does not save us from an angry God;

rather, He reveals the true heart of God, which is that of a loving Father—our True Father.

In John 14, Jesus is preparing the disciples for His departure from earth. He talks about how He is going to be with the Father and how He will return for them, in order to bring them to the Father as well. He then makes this powerful, yet confusing statement: "You know the way to the place where I am going."

Thomas (as well as the other disciples, I'm sure) was a bit confused by this. "Jesus, we don't even know where you're going," he said. "How are we supposed to know the way."

"I AM the way!" Jesus replied. He went on to tell them that He was the only way to the Father, and that they had, in fact, already seen the Father. This only served to confuse them further.

"Jesus, show us the Father. That will be enough for us if you will just do that," Phillip petitioned.

"After all this time, do you not know who I am?" Jesus replied. "If you've seen Me, you've seen the Father!"

I know this is a loose paraphrase, but catch what Jesus is saying here: *If you've seen Me, you've seen the Father.*

Jesus is the exact representation of who the Father is—in human form. God is not angry or distant; God is like Jesus. When we look at the life of Jesus, it gives us clues as to who God is. We know that God is immutable (He cannot change), and that God is perfectly revealed in Jesus. Jesus does not present a nicer version of God; Jesus reveals who God has been all along. Colossians 1 tells us that Jesus is the image of the invisible God (v. 15) and God was pleased to have everything that He is dwell in Jesus (v. 19).

Before I knew that God is like Jesus, I typically walked away from reading the Bible thinking that He was mad at me. And it's very easy to do that if you don't read the Bible correctly. You can't just take everything from the Bible at face value; you have to understand the full context of The Story. When I used to read even the New Testament, I thought that God was mad at me, because I didn't understand His heart.

If we only get our ideas about God from the Old Testament, we might view Him as a sadistic monster who delights in killing His enemies. Which is why we must go on to read the whole story. God is fully revealed in Jesus, who chose to die an unjust, violent death over killing His enemies. In fact, right before He died, Jesus asked the Father to forgive the people who killed Him!

So what do we do with all of the violence in the Old Testament? I can tell you that we can't simply ignore it, or perhaps highlight over those verses in Sharpie. There is an appropriate way to deal with them, but it is far more than what I can explain here. Whether or not you know how to explain the violence in the Old Testament is not the point. Our faith is not about defending the Bible; our faith is about knowing Jesus.

But what about the time when Jesus flipped over the tables in the temple?

That's an excellent question. This story is found in all four Gospels, and is usually brought up when discussing this issue, because it's one of the most (and only) physically violent acts that Jesus did in the New Testament. You've probably heard the story, so I'll summarize it by saying that the leaders of the temple—who were supposed to be God's representatives—were very corrupt; they blatantly did things that kept the common man from gaining access to God. (This was before the cross, which gave each of us personal access to God without the assistance of an earthly mediator.) So in explaining this act of violence, we must look at the context of who Jesus was dealing with: religious leaders who were supposed to represent God to the people, but were instead preventing the people from getting to God.

God is like Jesus. God has always been like Jesus. We haven't always known this to be true, but now we do. ~ Brian Zahnd

Day 10 † God Is Like Jesus

Questions

1) Do you feel like God is mad at you?

2) If you answered "yes" to the previous question, what do you think made you feel this way? Did you come to this conclusion on your own, or did someone tell you that God is mad at you?

3) Do you find it easier to trust God now that you know that He is like Jesus? Why or why not?

Activation

Read John 14:1-12. Then, ponder these verses from the Old Testament:

For his anger lasts only a moment, but his favor lasts a lifetime; weeping may stay for the night, but rejoicing comes in the morning.
~ Psalm 30:5

Who is a God like you, who pardons sin and forgives the transgression of the remnant of his inheritance? You do not stay angry forever but delight to show mercy. ~ Micah 7:18

Here we see David and the Prophet Micah catching glimpses of who God truly is, long before He was fully revealed in Jesus. Can you see how God has always been like Jesus, even amidst the confusing violence of the Old

Testament? Perhaps you can, or perhaps you are still struggling with the idea that God is like Jesus.

Sometimes, when you've been taught a lie for most of your life, it can be very difficult to unlearn it. And if you've been told for years that God is mad at you, I don't expect what I have to say to instantly erase that. But what I do know is that the Holy Spirit has the power to reveal things to your heart that I cannot. Remain sensitive to Him and allow Him to talk to you about this today.

This idea may not seem important to you, but it is crucial. God has deposited greatness inside of each one of us, and He wants to draw it out of us. This is what we mean when we say we are to "become like Christ"—we are to grow into the very nature that He has deposited inside of us. But this will not happen if we cannot trust God, and we cannot trust God when we feel that He is mad at us.

It's okay if all of this theology seems over your head. It's a complex idea, and I'm only scratching the surface. I feel as though I've only given you a small piece of the puzzle, but I'm okay with that, because I want you to study and think about it for yourself. This is one of those things that you will not fully understand just by hearing me talk about it; you need to experience it for yourself.

DAY 11
THE FATHER'S HEART

Last year, I was working as an executive assistant at a hospital on the other side of town when a stray chihuahua wandered into our parking lot. One of the maintenance guys pointed him out to me, and I knew immediately that I wanted to take him home. When my boss—the hospital CEO—walked by moments later, I was holding a dirty, terrified, extra small dog in my arms. Eight hours later, this dog was wrapped in a surgical blanket on the floor of his Mercedes-Benz as we drove home.

That night, I arrived home in the middle of a thunderstorm with my new friend, Enoch. I took him inside, gave him a bath, and wrapped him in a warm blanket. As I held my shivering, 4-lb. friend close to my chest, I began to think about my True Father.

You see, at some point you and I were a lot like Enoch—dirty, malnourished, wandering through life, in search of home. In the middle of our mess, the Father picked us up and held us in His arms, and He didn't care what anyone thought about Him for doing so. He brought us home, cleaned us up, gave us a new name, and adopted us as His own.

As the days turned into weeks, Enoch went from being fearful and cautious to bold and confident. Rather than cowering in the corner, he enjoyed the run of the entire house. I remember when he learned that he could go up and down the stairs. Now, I'll be in my office in the back corner of the second floor, and I'll hear the tag on his collar jingling as he climbs the stairs and comes bounding down the hallway to find me.

Every time I look at Enoch, I'm reminded of the heart of the Father. Every time he comes into my office, puts his paws up on my leg, and stares at me with his wide eyes, I catch a glimpse of myself. I'm the one who was wandering through the parking lot, dirty and alone. I'm the one who was rescued. I'm the one who was cleaned up. I'm the one who was adopted. I'm the one who puts my paws up on my Dad's leg, begging to be picked up one more time.

When Enoch wants to sit on my lap while I'm working, honestly, it's a major inconvenience. But once I pick him up and sit him down on my lap, once he falls asleep and begins to snore gently, it's totally worth it. And I think that's the way God feels about us. I think a lot of the time when we think we're "helping" Him, we're actually making His job more complicated. But He doesn't mind; He just wants to be with us.

I've talked about a lot of the high points; but at times, Enoch is obnoxious. Sometimes, he makes messes. But I've never once reconsidered my decision to adopt him. And here's the thing: I don't just tolerate him—he brings me joy, even amidst the mess.

That's exactly how the Father feels about you. You bring Him joy, even in the middle of your mess. When you're "helping" Him, He doesn't care that you're slowing Him down, because He just wants to be with you.

That's the Father's heart. He came to you, and He continues to come to you. He chose you, and He doesn't regret it. He adopted you, and He continues to adopt you.

I know Enoch is just a dog, but to me, he's a picture of the Father. Except he's me, and I'm the father. My family likes to joke that Enoch has gone from being an orphan to being entitled. But you know what? I would rather him have an entitlement mentality—because he knows who he is—than an orphaned heart.

Many of our churches today are full of spiritual orphans. They're in the house, but they don't feel as though they belong in the house. Which do you think the Father would rather have? Orphans who show up to church on Sundays, do their part, give faithfully, but never catch the Father's heart, that never learn that everything in the house is theirs? Or would He rather have sons and daughters, who perhaps become a bit entitled at times, but only because they realize that everything the Father has is theirs?

He meant us to see Him and live with Him and draw our life from His smile. ~ A.W. Tozer

Questions

1) Have you ever caught a glimpse of the Father's heart for you personally? If so, what did you see?
2) Do you feel as though you live most of your life as a spiritual orphan or as a child of the King?

Activation

How blessed is God! And what a blessing he is! He's the Father of our Master, Jesus Christ, and takes us to the high places of blessing in him. Long before he laid down earth's foundations, he had us in mind, had settled on us as the focus of his love, to be made whole and holy by his love. Long, long ago he decided to adopt us into his family through Jesus Christ (What pleasure he took in planning this!) He wanted us to enter into the celebration of his lavish gift-giving by the hand of his beloved son. ~ Ephesians 1:3-6, MSG

Ask the Father to reveal your true identity as a son or daughter to you on a deeper level. Remember, this is an ongoing process that often happens in layers. As you begin to peel back the layers of your orphaned heart your true self and identity in Christ will begin to emerge.

I love what John Eldredge says in the foreword to Brady Boyd's book *Sons and Daughters: Spiritual Orphans Finding Their Way Home:* "Even though we are sons and daughters, we still perceive ourselves and our lives through a very different set of lenses." He goes on to say, "I am still an infant in these matters; the longest strides I've taken toward sonship have been only in the last six months."

From my perspective, if anyone should "get it," it's John Eldredge. He has taught on this topic for years, written a bunch of books about knowing the Father; so to find out that he is still stumbling toward the starting line is quite liberating. No matter how much we think we know, we're just getting started in this thing of knowing the Father. Yet, we can be confident that He knows us, and that He sees us crossing the finish line in victory, even while we're still trying to figure out where to begin.

DAY 12
PARADIGM OF SCARCITY

During World War II, a German invasion of Italy caused common household items to suddenly become very scarce. This led to many people going to extreme circumstances to acquire basic items that we can purchase freely today from our local Walmart. These events caused many people to develop a *paradigm of scarcity*.

A paradigm of scarcity is rooted in the belief that there is only a limited amount of resources out there, so we must fight to get what we need before it's too late. It causes us to hoard ridiculous quantities of things, or put things away and refuse to use them for fear that we might need them someday and have no way to obtain them.

This is the very principle that was at play in the Parable of the Talents, which is found in Luke 19. While everyone else was out multiplying what had been given to them, one man took what he had and buried it in the sand, because he was afraid.

A few weeks ago, I was at one of my favorite coffee houses, which is located in Oklahoma City. It's a long drive from my house, so I purchased a bag of artisan coffee beans to take home. They were a bit more expensive than the coffee beans I normally buy, but that didn't bother me, because I knew they would taste a lot better. When I returned home, however, I noticed that I was intentionally using less ground coffee than normal each time I brewed a cup. This resulted in my coffee being weaker, even tasting watery. My reasoning was I needed to make my "good" coffee last longer, whereas if it were average coffee, I could brew it at normal strength.

When you live out of a paradigm of scarcity, it causes you to take what is yours and bury it so that you cannot access it, or only access a portion of it. Sometimes, that looks like taking a talent and burying it in the sand; other times, it looks like watering down your coffee to the point where you're drinking it but not actually enjoying it. Can you see how a paradigm of scarcity traps you in a place where you settle for less than you were created for?

I was listening to Erwin McManus—who pastors a church in Los Angeles—give a talk the other day, and he was speaking on the topic of living life intentionally. He told us that humans are the only creatures that are capable of living for less than they were created for. Dogs fully experience being a dog, cats fully experience being a cat, but humans don't always experience what being fully human is like, because our false selves get in the way.

McManus went on to ask a series of powerful questions. *Have you ever wondered how someone can be so famous, yet end their life? So wealthy, but drink themselves to death? So famous, but living a nightmare?*

We often think that if we get to the point where we finally have _____, our lives will make sense and everything will be okay, but that is a lie. Because you can obtain everything you ever wanted, yet still live for less than you were created for.

When you realize that everything you have comes from God and God will provide everything you need, it sets you free to live with open hands. But before you can give, you must receive—because when you don't know how to receive, you'll take what you're given and bury it.

Today, I am brewing my artisan coffee from the coffee house in Oklahoma City at full strength. Finally, I can enjoy it in the way that it was intended to be enjoyed. And guess what? The bag isn't empty yet. And when it is, I know where I can get more.

Many people are unsatisfied in life because they live with a paradigm of scarcity. We were not meant to go through life guarding, protecting, and fighting for what is ours; we were meant to live with open hearts and open hands, knowing that the infinite resources of Heaven are available to us. I'm not just talking about material possessions, though that is a part of it. I don't believe in the so-called "prosperity gospel," but I do agree with 1 Timothy 6:17, which says that God *richly provides us with everything for our enjoyment.* And I also know that the first part of that verse calls us to be generous, to stay humble when we've been successful in this life, and to never put our hope in money, but to trust in God instead.

> *Freely you have received; freely give.*
> ~ *Jesus, Matthew 10:8*

Questions

1) Do you often fear that there will never be enough, or are you able to trust God to provide everything you need?

2) Have you ever gotten something that you really wanted and still felt empty inside? Why do you think you felt that way?

3) Do you feel that you are living at the level you were created for? Why or why not?

Activation

The orphan heart and paradigm of scarcity are closely related. That is why we've been talking so much about getting our hearts back, becoming sons and daughters, and learning to trust God, so we can live with open hearts and hands.

I believe that breaking free from the orphan heart and paradigm of scarcity is a two-part process. There is a part that only God can play and a part that only we can play. God sets us free, but we must still be intentional to walk away from the destructive ways of thinking and living that have kept us enslaved. In my case, this was as simple as choosing to enjoy my coffee at full strength.

If you find yourself living with an orphaned heart or from a paradigm of scarcity, what are some practical things that you can do to break free? (Remember, only God can set you free, but you also need to take action once He sets you free. For me, it was choosing to not water down my coffee any longer. It is sometimes that easy, but most of the time, it will be far more complex.)

I wish there was a formula that I could give you for how to overcome these things, but there are some things you only learn by doing. You will likely need to talk to God about this, think it over for a while, and then come up with some practical steps for walking away from this inferior way of living, so that you can access all that you were created for.

DAY 13
FULLY CONVINCED

A few years ago, I was having a conversation with my friend Annie when she asked me about a particular theological topic: the role of the Holy Spirit in convicting believers of sin. At the time, Annie had recently spoken with a friend who had adopted a sort of new theology (new to Annie, at least) that the role of the Holy Spirit is more about comforting us than convicting us of sin. Annie's friend had been taught the opposite for much of her life, but after reading the Bible for herself, she claimed she couldn't find any verses that talked about the Spirit convicting believers of sin.

"What do you think?" Annie asked me.

"Of course the Spirit convicts us of sin," I replied.

"I agree. Do you know of a Scripture that backs that up?"

I had to think about that one for a moment.

"I'm not sure where it is in Scripture, but I know that He *does*," I replied.

It seemed right, and that's what I had been taught for much of my life. But when I really thought about it, I had no idea where it was in the Bible—or if it was even in the

Bible at all. So, I started searching for a verse about the Holy Spirit convicting believers of sin. The only problem was, I couldn't find one. Well, there was *one,* but it didn't say what I wanted it to say. The whole experience was quite frustrating.

Right before Jesus went to the cross, He pulled His disciples aside and told them that Someone better than Him—the Holy Spirit—would come not long after He left. Then, He told them that the Spirit would convict them of their righteousness, rather than their sin.

And he [the Holy Spirit], when He comes, will convict the world concerning sin and righteousness and judgment; concerning sin, because they do not believe in Me; and concerning righteousness, because I go to the Father and you no longer see Me; and concerning judgment, because the ruler of this world has been judged ~ John 16:8-11, NASB, brackets mine.

This is the one Scripture I was talking about—the one that didn't say what I wanted it to say. Unfortunately for my preconceived notions, this is the only Scripture that comes close to saying that the Spirit convicts believers of sin.

From the above text, you'll see that the Holy Spirit convicts of three things: sin, righteousness, and judgment. It's very easy to breeze through the first part of this and think that the Spirit's role is to convict *us* of these three things. In reality, John goes on to talk about the three unique groups that the Spirit's conviction is aimed toward. If you slow down and simply *read* the text, you'll catch it— no knowledge of the original Greek language required!

1) Sin

Who does the Spirit convict of sin?

... *concerning sin, because they do not believe in Me.*

Jesus is the one talking here, so we can see that those who do not believe in Jesus are the ones that the Spirit convicts of sin. This is consistent with numerous Scriptures that talk about us not being able to come to Jesus without the Spirit first revealing our need for Him.

We know that this verse does not refer to believers, because Jesus was talking to the disciples, and He said "because *they* do not believe in Me," not "because *you* do not believe in Me."

2) Righteousness

Again, the text points to a specific group of people.

... *concerning righteousness, because I go to the Father, and you no longer see Me.*

It's quite clear that this second work of the Holy Spirit is targeted at the group that Jesus was talking to. We've already established that Jesus was talking to the disciples, to *those who believe in Him*. This means that the Spirit's conviction of righteousness applies to us as well, because we believe in Jesus.

When the Spirit reveals our need for a Savior and we come to Jesus, He exchanges the death in us for the life in Him. The theological term for this is *righteousness*. But we don't always feel or even believe we are righteous, do we? Many of us are still trying to unlearn the ways of the bad father, and embrace the ways of our True Father.

The word *convict* that is used in John 16 simply means to *fully convince*. Jesus said the Spirit would fully convince believers that they are righteous *because I go to the Father, and you no longer see Me*.

I don't think the disciples needed to be convinced that they were righteous when Jesus was right there with them. But what about when He hung naked on the cross, a picture of a failed Messiah? That's when they got scared. That's when they wondered if everything they had believed in was really just a wishful fairy tale. They weren't convinced that Jesus would rise from the dead, even though He had told them beforehand. In their minds, the crucifixion was a picture that Jesus had failed—and it was, for a moment.

If only the disciples had access to the Spirit then. Not only were they not fully convinced of their righteousness, they weren't even fully convinced that the person they had been following really was the Savior of the world.

We know what happens next. Jesus was taken off the cross and put in the grave. After three days, the Father raised Him from the dead, proving that He was not just another failed revolutionary who claimed to be the Messiah. He then appeared to the disciples, and they hung out together for a few weeks before He ascended to the Father's side, where He remains today.

Because we walk by faith rather than by sight, because we believe in Someone we cannot see or feel or touch, because Jesus isn't physically present with us to remind us that we are righteous, we need the Spirit to convict—fully convince—us of our righteousness.

If you have a relationship with Jesus, you are already righteous, regardless of whatever messes you're still trying to clean up. It is crucial that we open our hearts to the Spirit and allow Him to convince us of this reality, because there is a bad father who wants to convince us that what God has done in our hearts is somehow insufficient.

3) Judgment

... concerning judgment, because the ruler of this world has been judged.

Here we see that God's judgment is aimed not at believers, but at the *ruler of this world*—the bad father.

<u>Now</u> judgment is upon this world; <u>now</u> the ruler of this world will be cast out. ~ John 12:31, NASB

The purpose of the Spirit's conviction of judgment is to fully convince us that the lies of the bad father that often torment us will someday cease. Now, his power has been stripped away. Someday, he won't be able to lie to us at all anymore. We will fully know and comprehend the truth of who God says we are, and the truth will set us free. This reality has yet to fully manifest in our world, but we can experience today what is yet to come and live as if it were already true—because it is.

The Father loves you. Jesus has finished His work. The Spirit has come. You have nothing to fear. ~ Alan Smith

Questions

1) How has today's discussion changed the way you view the role of the Holy Spirit in your life?

2) Do you find these changes easy to accept or challenging? Why do you think that is?

3) What are some of the ways that the bad father has been telling you that you aren't righteous?

4) What do you know to be *most* true about you, based on what Jesus has done and who He says you are?

Activation

Today, allow the Holy Spirit to convince you that you are righteous. You need this, because there is a bad father telling you that you are not.

There may be contrary evidence in your life to the reality that you are righteous, but that is not what is *most* true about you. When you begin to embrace who you *already* are and live out of that place, that stuff has a way of working itself out.

If you are hearing an accusing voice, it's not the voice of the Spirit. The Spirit is gentle and kind. He reminds us of who we are, that God has a better way for us, that we belong to the King, that our failures no longer define us.

The Spirit will not ignore your sin, but His aim is never to make you feel guilty or ashamed. Instead, He tries to get you to see who you already are (because of what Jesus has done), so that you will no longer be content to live for less than you were created for. Because when you sin, you are living out of your false self; you are settling for less than you were created for.

DAY 14
BE LOVE.

Above all else, we were created for love. We were created to love God and be loved by God, to receive His love and to give it away. Unfortunately, the concept of love has become so twisted and distorted in our culture that many of us have no idea what it means to receive pure, selfless love—let alone give it away. But we cannot love unless we first receive love, and we cannot even receive God's love on our own; He has to help us.

I pray that you, being rooted and established in love, may have power, together with all the Lord's holy people, to grasp how wide and long and high and deep is the love of God, and to know this love that surpasses knowledge—that you may be filled to the measure of all the fullness of God. ~ Ephesians 3:17b-19

Over the past year, I've become familiar with a guy named Bob Goff, who lives in San Diego. Bob works as a construction lawyer in Seattle, but he is also in the full-time ministry of loving people. Literally, his primary focus is loving people, and after reading his book, *Love Does,* it's obvious that his strategy is changing the world around him. I believe that if we all did this, if we all learned how to love one another—or at least attempted to love one another—this world would look a lot different than it does now.

Being love doesn't just mean that we love our family and friends, though that is a part of it. Being love is about loving everyone we come into contact with—those who are like us, those who aren't like us, even our worst enemies. But there is another element of being love that involves far more intentional action. This looks like feeding the homeless on Saturday mornings, tutoring a junior high student after school on Tuesdays, leading a small group at your church, coordinating a food drive to benefit a local food bank, being a part of a community service project, going overseas on a mission trip, or something else entirely.

Being love is simple; just get out there and do something! But it's more than just something you do on the weekends; we can be love in the context of our Monday-Friday lives as well. The reason why I mentioned going overseas on a mission trip last is because I want to highlight the reality that there are plenty of opportunities to be love right here in our own backyards.

Love doesn't have to be complicated to be genuine and make an impact. It can be as simple as giving an encouraging word to a friend, or the clerk at Walmart who

73

looks like they've had a rough day. Whenever I go to a fast food restaurant or department store, I make an effort to look the clerk in the eye, call them by name, and make their day a little brighter. This may seem insignificant, but it's these small actions that eventually lead to big actions as love begins to overtake us. A lot of people want to do big things for God, but how will you get there if you can't even love the people who are in front of you each and every day?

The world around us is crying out to know the Father. And when we live to be love, we give them a glimpse of the Father's heart. We have found the love that we have been longing for all of our lives. Now, the time has come to give it away. This is what we were created for—to receive love, and to be love.

We don't need to keep auditioning for the parts we've all been cast for. Don't wait for permission; go love people. ~ Bob Goff

Questions

1) Do you feel like you are full of the love of God and can give it away? Why or why not?

2) Are you currently "being love" on a regular basis, wherever you are? If so, what can you do to take it to the next level? If not, what's stopping you?

3) Are you currently doing something "extra" to reach out to others in your community in your spare time? Why or why not?

4) What can you do to create some margin in your life to serve your community?

Activation

Today, make an effort to look for people who you can love on purpose. It may be as simple as a smile and encouraging word. God may even put something specific on your heart that relates to a specific situation a person is going through. Sometimes you are aware of this situation; other times, you are not. When God speaks something to you about another person that you didn't previously know, it's called a *word of knowledge*.

Don't be afraid to ask God to give you a word of knowledge for someone you will encounter today. It may sound intimidating, but anyone can do it. You may be thinking, "But I don't have that spiritual gift," but this is something *anyone* can do, because all it entails is hearing from God and speaking what He says to someone else. Hearing God doesn't have to be a mystical experience or an audible voice; often, it's simply a strong impression in your heart. In fact, when God gives me a word for a specific person, my heart usually begins to burn within me (like a rush of adrenaline), and that's usually how I know it's really God that is talking to me.

Don't be afraid of looking foolish, or even getting it wrong. If you do not allow yourself the freedom to fail, you won't succeed in being love. Sometimes love is raw and messy, but that's okay. Love doesn't have to be perfect, just as long as it's sincere.

As I was talking to a friend the other day, he began to tell me that there are many things in life that we're not ever really "ready" for; we just have to do them anyway. The example that he used was that you're never really *ready* to have kids, and if you wait until you are, it will never happen. Being love is kind of the same way. If you wait until you think you're good at it, you'll never do it. We learn how to be love in the process of being love. So if you're afraid, relax. We're *all* afraid of things. Fear rarely goes away until you make the choice to move forward in spite of it. Why not take a risk and be love to someone today?

In the words of Bob Goff: *If you fail, then fail at the right stuff—fail trying, not watching.*

DAY 15
POWERFUL AND FREE

I've been around the church world long enough to notice a certain trend. While it mostly affects teenagers and young adults, people of all ages wrestle with this—to find their *purpose*, to find *God's will* for their life. I have noticed many people get quite exhausted trying to accomplish this, as if God's will for your life is something that He makes really difficult for you to figure out. But that's the way we think, isn't it?

I believe that God has a calling on my life. I believe that part of that calling looks like me being in a specific city, doing a specific thing at some point. But right now, I know I'm doing exactly what I'm supposed to be doing vocationally, working as a freelance writer for a web development firm and automotive advertisement agency. In my free time, I write materials for ministries and do other projects, such as this devotional. I know that I'm called to do the latter, but the former is just something I do to make money right now. I enjoy it, but I am definitely not as passionate about it as I am writing books.

About a year ago, I was on a road trip in Oklahoma. I had brought my digital camera with me and was doing a little photography, just for fun. I ended up in the town of Durant, where I decided to stop and photograph a few historic buildings on the downtown square. As I was doing this, a local business owner saw me and struck up a conversation. Turns out, he was looking for someone to write some content for him. He even offered me a paid project to work on that very day.

You know what I didn't say in that moment?

I don't know; let me pray about it.

No! I just did it. And I had no idea that it was God opening a door at the time. For all I knew, it was another side project I didn't need to get involved in, as I was a week away from starting the job as executive assistant to the CEO at the hospital.

Four months later, I realized the executive assistant job wasn't my thing, so I took a leap of faith and began working part-time for the guy that I had met on the street in Oklahoma. At first, I didn't pray about it; I just started making plans. I knew that something had to change with my current job, and I also knew that the responsibility was ultimately mine to make that change.

I used to think that because I'm a Christian, God had to specifically approve everything I did, right down to the smallest details. But then I realized it didn't quite work that way. The Bible tells us that if we're able to work, we need to do so in order to provide for ourselves and our families. But the Bible doesn't tell us *where* to work, when to change jobs, or if we even should change jobs. That is why we must have a relationship with God, and allow Him to speak to us. I have felt God leading me toward some of the jobs I have held, but there have been others that I took simply because I needed a job.

After I had lined up the new job with the guy from Oklahoma, I brought it up to the CEO. I wanted him to tell me what he thought I should do, but he instead told me that the choice was mine to make; I could leave or I could stay.

When I prayed about it, I didn't feel God giving me a definite answer either way. In fact, all I could really hear was that I didn't need to be afraid of not having enough money if I did change jobs. This was my greatest concern, since the new job would pay far less to start.

Isn't it interesting how God speaks exactly what we need to hear? He doesn't always give us the "do this" answer we often look for, but I think it's because He wants us to trust Him.

After I quit my job at the hospital, things weren't immediately perfect. The new job was very uncomfortable for the first month, but things began to look up from there. Now, six months have passed, and I am making the same amount of money that I made at the hospital, and I work from home instead of commuting to the other side of town. Looking back, I can see God's fingerprints all over my journey, but I didn't see what He was doing at the time.

God did not tell me to take a random road trip to Oklahoma. He did not tell me to stop in the town I stopped in. He did, however, ensure that my new boss and I crossed paths at the perfect moment. With all of this set up, wouldn't God have told me to take the guy up on his job offer? Why did He give me the freedom to make the choice myself? What if I would have missed it?

God is powerful. He is an initiator. We were made in His image. In the beginning, God told Adam to name the animals, but He didn't give him any further direction. Whatever Adam decided to name them, that was their name. God is powerful, but He doesn't use His power to control us. Instead, He empowers us to control ourselves. You may have already noticed, but there is this fruit of the Spirit called *self-control*. Isn't it interesting that an evidence of the Spirit's work in your life is that you're able to make your own decisions and take ownership of the consequences—good or bad?

I'm not saying that you shouldn't pray, ask for direction, or seek God's input on your plans. If He tells you to do something specific, you need to do it. But if you don't feel Him leading you in a specific direction, remember that He made you powerful and free. You have been given the mind of Christ. You are capable of making good decisions. You are able to accept responsibility if things go wrong, and if this does happen, God is more than capable of getting you back on the right path.

When Jesus called the disciples, they weren't frantically searching for God's will, nor were they sitting quietly on the couch doing nothing, waiting for a voice. Jesus called the disciples in the context of their everyday lives, when they least expected it.

Questions

1) How has today's discussion challenged you?

2) Has anything changed in the way you view your role and God's role in the process of decision making? What has changed and why?

3) Do you truly feel powerful and free, or do you feel that God is trying to control you? Why do you think you feel this way?

Activation

For God hath not given us the spirit of fear; but of power, and of love, and of a sound mind. ~ 2 Timothy 1:7, KJV

Here we see that God has made us powerful and given us a sound mind. But also notice what the text says God has *not* given us: a spirit of fear.

There is no fear in love. But perfect love drives out fear, because fear has to do with punishment. The one who fears is not made perfect in love. ~ 1 John 4:18

God has not given us a spirit of fear, but has instead given us a spirit of love. However, we are not made perfect (or *complete*) in that love as long as we are living in fear. There is a difference between having thoughts of fear from time to time (which is a normal part of life) and living in constant fear, and we know that God's love takes care of both. He heals our hearts, so that we can live free from constant fear, and He also takes care of the fears that arise as we move through life.

Some say that the opposite of fear is *faith*, but I have heard that it is actually *love*, because it is love that drives out fear. If this is true, all we have to do when we feel afraid is ask God to remind us of how He feels about us.

God has given you a sound mind. You can trust your heart. You don't have to live in fear of missing what God has for you. You may not see Him working in your life now, but when you get further along on the journey, you'll look back and see His fingerprints everywhere.

DAY 16
MORE THAN THE ROLES YOU PLAY

I play a lot of roles in my life. I'm a writer, editor, social media manager, volunteer at my church, youth ministry worker, aspiring theologian, wanna-be community activist, son, friend, mentor, chihuahua owner, and much more.

You probably have a long list of roles that you play as well, and an even longer list of roles that you'd like to play if you had the time. When you assemble your list in your head, what matters the most to you?

For me, the stuff relating to my family and friends is the most important. The rest of the stuff, not so much. Sure, I enjoy writing, editing, youth ministry, and all of those other things, but when I make those roles my primary pursuits, they usually end up leaving me feeling empty.

There is something more—something greater—than all of these roles that I play: my identity as a child of the King. My true self has more to do with that identity than all of the roles I play. If someone were to say that I'm a writer, it would be true in a sense, but it's not what defines me. When you make your identity primarily about a role that you play rather than your identity in Christ, you will always find yourself coming up empty.

The roles that I play are an important part of my life, but I don't look to those roles to tell me who I am, because I know that they are too small. To say that I am a youth ministry worker, while it is true, is far too restrictive. Not that I am discontent in this area, but I know that my primary identity is in the God who created the universe in a matter of words. He is so much bigger than any of the roles that I play, so why would I want to limit what He says about me to those roles? If I did that, I could miss out on another role that He has for me later on in life, because I've already decided that I am the roles I'm playing right now and I will always be those roles.

When you look to the roles that you play to tell you who you are, you will end up forgetting who you are when those roles change. But if you look to your True Father to tell you who you are, your identity will remain consistent through the ups and downs of life—through every transition and change, every valley and every storm. And when your identity is in the Father, He knows that He can hand you a supporting role in His story, that He can take you from being a stage hand in the shadows to an actor in the spotlight. Ironically, He knows you can fulfill this role well, because you do anything but *act;* all you know to do is be yourself and pour out the life that He put inside of you while you were in the shadows.

I think there are a lot of people who run onstage and try to take on a part without spending time in the shadows, so they end up acting out whatever they think is best to act out instead of reading off the script—the script the Father was trying to teach them in the shadows. The script itself is not complicated or restrictive; the script simply tells us to love and serve people, and let God be the center of attention, because He is the star and it's His show.

No matter where you are in the process, whether in the shadows or in the spotlight, you are more than the roles you play. You can live with confidence even if you are working as an administrative assistant, running errands for the people whom you would rather be reciting the script alongside. Even if you never get called into the role you want, you are worth so much more than the greatest role you could ever play while on this earth.

In the eyes of your True Father, you are of infinite value; you are so much more than the roles you play.

Questions

1) What roles are you playing right now?

2) What roles would you like to play?

3)   What roles do you need to stop playing?

Activation

As you answer the questions above, they will help you map out where you are and what you should do to move forward. By listing the roles that you play, you will be able to get an "aerial view" of your life that you often don't see as you're moving through it. By listing the roles that you *want* to play, you're able to see how the life you're living does or does not align with the life you were meant to live.

Now comes the hard part. In order to begin playing the roles that you want to play most, you often have to give up some of the roles that you are currently playing. Part of this is for the sake of margin—you may have to give up a *good* role that you enjoy in order to make room for a *great* role you know you were created to play, a role that keeps you up at night, dreaming of what the future could be. The other part of this involves realizing that there are some roles you cannot play simultaneously. For example, you cannot play the role of someone who hides in fear and the role of someone who takes bold risks at the same time. You've got to decide what role you want to play most, what role you want to be remembered for playing.

I didn't get to it in the core of this discussion, but this brings up another side to the roles we play—a darker side.

Day 16 † More than the Roles You Play

There are many of us who, when we encounter the brokenness of the world, begin playing roles we were never intended to play. Some take on the role of a victim and attempt to manipulate others; some take on the role of an aggressor and release their wrath on the world. Both of these roles are just attempts to cover up internal pain, rather than dealing with it properly.

Perhaps you're afraid of what people will think of you. You want them to love and accept you, so you take on a role where you never say "no." You go through life playing this role, saying "yes" to everything and everyone. Even when everything inside of you wants to say "no," you continue to say "yes," because that is the role you think you must play. The sad thing is, many people never realize they are playing this role until their lives are on the brink of destruction.

A man stays at a dead-end job; a woman refuses to walk away from an abusive relationship. Somewhere along the line, they've been convinced that these are the roles they must play, that this is all there is. It isn't. There are other roles available, and you are more than the roles you play.

DAY 17
DESIRE

Do you like stories?

I do. In fact, I think I'll tell you one.

It was an overcast morning in Seattle as 17-year-old Michael walked into a diner near Pike Place Market. As he scanned the room, he noticed his mentor, 64-year-old Steve, sitting at a booth near the back.

"Michael!" Steve exclaimed when he saw him approaching. "How are you doing, man?"

"I'm okay," Michael said, slinking into the booth.

"Okay—what's up?" Steve asked abruptly. He often did this, skipping over the small talk in order to dive head-first into matters of the soul.

"Well ..." Michael began. "I was hanging out with Hannah last night ..." He paused, slightly longer this time. "And we, uh—"

"Had sex?" Steve asked nonchalantly as he took a sip of coffee.

Michael's face nearly turned white. "No!"

"Okay ..." Steve said, taking another sip of coffee. "So what happened?"

Michael was silent. "Well, we technically didn't have sex, but we came close."

"Okay ..." Steve said again, giving way to a long silence in their booth. "So why are you telling me this?"

"Because it was wrong, and you're my mentor ..."

"Was it?"

"What do you mean?"

"Was it wrong?" the old man asked, stroking his beard.

"Yes?"

"Why do you hesitate?"

"Well, it didn't feel wrong ..."

"And there you have it," Steve thought to himself. "You know, Michael," he said aloud.

Michael leaned in, knowing that Steve was about to impart some serious wisdom, as was his custom.

"Your desire isn't bad. In fact, it's very normal." He paused, noticing the look of confusion on Michael's face. "The problem is that your desire is not all there is. There are some deeper desires beneath it, which you have yet to realize. Those are the desires you need to pay attention to." Steve sat back in the booth, one eye on Michael, the other on his coffee mug. *Would this be an inappropriate time to take a sip?*

"I have no clue what you just said," Michael paused. "But I know it's important."

Steve chuckled.

"Help me understand," Michael appealed.

"Underneath that desire for sex is a deeper desire, a desire for love and affection—that's what you really crave. And if you don't have love and affection, there's no amount of sex that can ever satisfy you. If you chase after it, the life you want will always seem just out of reach. But if you focus on love, well, the sex is just a bonus—when you're married, of course."

Michael just stared at him, too stunned to speak. It was as if a veil that had blinded him from seeing the truth—from seeing what was true about him—was dropping from in front of his eyes.

"Your deeper desires tell you about your true identity," Steve continued. "But most people get it backward—they let their shallow desires tell them who they are, and ignore their deeper desires altogether. No wonder we have a bunch of kids running around like sex-crazy animals. They've believed a lie that tells them that is all they are, so all they know to do is act accordingly."

"So you're saying—" Michael closed his mouth abruptly, taking a moment to gather his thoughts. "I need to focus on love and affection from Hannah, rather than the, well, you know?"

"Close, but not quite. Say that part about love and affection again."

"I need to focus on getting love and affection from Hannah—"

"And that's where you're wrong," the old man said, a bit abrasively this time.

"How am I wrong?" Michael asked, too confused to be annoyed. "Isn't that what you told me to do?"

"I told you to focus on what you can *get* from her? How about what you can *give* to her?"

At that moment, another light bulb turned on in Michael's head. This is what he loved about the old man: he wasn't just wise; he went straight to the heart of the matter.

"Here's the deal, Mike. If you focus on another person as your source of love and affection, you're setting yourself up for disappointment. Have I ever loved you perfectly?"

"Well, you've definitely made a big impact on my life."

"Of course I haven't! And I'm never going to—but that doesn't mean I'm not going to try," he said, nearly choking up as the last phrase left his lips.

Silence filled the booth.

Staring down at his coffee, Steve slowly lifted his head. Michael was looking straight through him.

"Thank you." Tears were beginning to form in his eyes.

"Let God be your source, son. I'll disappoint you. Hannah will disappoint you. We're all going to disappoint you." His words were rich with emotion. "But God," he paused, tearing up a bit himself. "He never will."

From this story, we can see that the function of desire is often confusing. We think our shallow desires are what we are defined by, when they are really just intended to point us toward what we truly desire. It's not that we don't want the shallow desires at all; we often do, but they are only part of the story. Sometimes, our desires are in conflict with one another. When this happens, we often default to siding with the shallow desire. The deeper desire seems too far off, buried too deeply below the surface—or perhaps we don't know that we even *have* deeper desires.

I was at a church in Austin once, and the pastor was sharing his heart with us as he led into the Eucharist. He talked about how he had been reading Psalm 103 while watching the sun rise that morning.

Praise the LORD, my soul, and forget not all his benefits—who forgives all your sins and heals all your diseases, who redeems your life from the pit and crowns you with love and compassion, who satisfies your desires with good things so that your youth is renewed like the eagle's. ~ Psalm 103:2-5

"You know what I love about that last verse?" the pastor asked as he finished reading. "It says that God satisfies my desires with *good* things. Now, not everything I desire could be defined as *good things,* but when God satisfies my desires, He satisfies the good desires of my heart. He doesn't give me everything I want, and I'm grateful for that, but what He does give me is always good, because that's who He is."

There is an aspect of desire that we can fulfill ourselves, as you are probably aware of. But when God satisfies your desires, He digs beyond the surface, beyond your shallow desires, to your deeper desires—the things you truly desire. Those are the desires that He satisfies with good things. Those are the desires we must pay attention to.

Our shallow desires talk to us about what we think we need in the moment; our deeper desires talk to us about who we really are.

Questions

1) How has today's discussion changed the way you think about your desires?

2) Are there any desires that you once regarded as bad, but you now realize are just shallow?

3) What do you want? (It's not a trick question.) What do you *really* want?

4) How will you discover your deeper desires? How will you pursue them?

Activation

In certain Christian circles, we are often told that we need to kill our desires, because they are, for the most part, bad. The reasoning behind this line of thought varies, but at the end of the day, we think this way because we don't realize there are two types of desire. And when all we have to look at are our shallow desires, it's easy to see why we think the best option is to kill them. The problem with this is that Jesus cares deeply about our desires, and there is no scriptural basis for killing them. Sure, the Bible calls us to *take up our cross* and *crucify our flesh*, but does this really mean we are to give up desire altogether?

May he give you the desire of your heart and make all your plans succeed. ~ *Psalm 20:4*

You have granted him his heart's desire and have not withheld the request of his lips. ~ *Psalm 21:2*

Take delight in the LORD, and he will give you the desires of your heart. ~ *Psalm 37:4*

He fulfills the desires of those who fear him; he hears their cry and saves them. ~ *Psalm 145:19*

I think you get the point I am trying to make. Your heart is not bad; therefore, its desires are not bad. The desires of your heart are your deeper desires. The shallow desires aren't a part of the good heart that your True Father gave you. They are cheap imitations left over from the days of the bad father. They belong to the darkness, not the light, but they can still be used to point us toward the light, toward what we truly desire. If our deeper desires reveal what is true about us, it is fair to say that our shallow desires reveal what is *not* true about us. However, if we discard them, we may never discover our deeper desires, because our shallow desires are often fragments of our deeper desires, signposts that can guide us toward what we long for the most.

The journey toward unearthing your deeper desires is often a difficult and painful process. We don't settle for shallow desires because we prefer them; we settle for shallow desires because it's easy. We don't usually make the decision to ignore our deeper desires consciously; many of us don't even realize that we *have* deeper desires. When we begin to ask the tough questions, that is often when we begin to feel the most pain, because our souls are opened and exposed—we feel as though for all the world to see. When this happens, the normal reaction is to turn and run as fast as you can in the opposite direction. Looking past the junk of your shallow desires to find out what you truly desire can be a bit unnerving, but if we stay engaged, we will reap the rewards. Perhaps this is a part of what Jesus meant by *take up your cross*. Because when He took up His cross, it was difficult and painful, but the glory of the resurrection was on the other side.

Honestly, the only practical steps I can give you are a few questions to ask, which are on the previous page. There is not a formula for unearthing your deeper desires, just questions you can begin asking yourself and God. These questions are your tools. It's kind of like a treasure hunt—there are a lot of tools that you can utilize, but there is no formula for finding buried treasure. (If you are presented with one, you should probably be suspicious of it.)

You don't have to settle for shallow desires, and why would you want to? You can know your deeper desires, and you can press through the pain it may take to get to that place—the place of knowing what you really want.

May the Lord hear your cry as you long to discover the true desires of your heart. May He unearth your deepest desires and satisfy them with good things. May He captivate you with His unfailing love, forever and always, unto eternity. Amen.

DAY 18
OVERLAP OF THE AGES

If you follow the storyline of the Bible, you can see that it has a clear beginning and ending. It begins with God creating the world, followed shortly thereafter by the fall of man, and ends with God making all things new. In the middle, the world is terribly broken. Jesus comes back to fix it, but leaves halfway through the story, though not without a promise to send the Holy Spirit to be with us until He comes back to finish making all things new. In theological terms, this beginning and ending of the storyline mark two separate ages: *this present age* and *the age to come*. But there is also a point where the two ages overlap, a point where the realities of both ages are true simultaneously.

Sounds a bit awkward, doesn't it?

We live in the overlap of the ages.

Through His death on the cross, Jesus triumphed over death itself and began the age to come, which is the Kingdom of God. Yet, this present age has not yet passed away; the full reality of the Kingdom is yet to come. This is what we mean when we say the Kingdom is *now*, but *not yet*.

Think of it in terms of our presidential elections here in the United States: We elect a new president in November, but he or she doesn't take office until January. Through the cross, Jesus has already become the True King of the world, just as God is our True Father. But there are still others—imposters—claiming their perceived right to the throne. And so, while we know that Jesus is the True King of the world, we do not yet see that reality fully manifested on earth. We know it is fully manifested in Heaven, where Jesus is seated at the right hand of the Father, but meanwhile, here on earth, we've still got a bunch of pseudo-kings running around making a mess of things.

When Jesus taught His disciples how to pray in Matthew 6, one of the first things He taught them was, *your kingdom come, your will be done, on earth as it is in heaven.*

In other words, Jesus taught His disciples to pray that the reality of the age to come would begin to invade this present age. When this happens, the overlap of the ages begins to grow smaller, as life swallows up death and the reality of the Kingdom of God becomes *more true* on earth, just as it is already *fully true* in Heaven.

Not only did the disciples pray for this to happen, they soon began to become the answer to their own prayers. Jesus went up, the Holy Spirit came down, and really cool stuff started to happen as the disciples began to preach that the Kingdom of God had arrived.

If this sounds a bit controversial to you, that's because it is! In fact, many of the disciples who testified that the Kingdom of God had arrived were ultimately executed at the hands of the religious and political leaders of the day. These are the pseudo-kings, the rulers of this present age. The overlap of the ages is messy, because the Kingdom of God is conflicting with the kingdoms of this world, and the Kingdom of love and peace is foundationally different than the kingdoms of power and control.

The disciples got in trouble, because they believed and testified that the overlap of the ages had occurred, that the age to come had both *arrived* and *was arriving*. A theology about people going to Heaven when they die isn't very controversial, because it allows the kingdoms of this world to remain in control here on earth. But a Kingdom that comes down from Heaven and gives life to the world conflicts with the kingdoms of this world that seek to find life by imparting death into others. We are shifting from a kingdom that brings life to a select few at the expense of others to a Kingdom that—through the death of God in Christ—gives life to all who believe, while at the same time toppling the thrones of the rulers of this present age who have no idea what the way of sacrificial love and peace looks like.

We've been talking a lot about things that are *true* and things that are *more true*. This present age is true, but the age to come is more true. Slowly but surely, the overlap is growing smaller, until the day where it will no longer exist and all we will experience is the age to come.

I realize that today's discussion is a bit more complex than previous discussions. However, I also realize that not everything is simple in the Kingdom; there are some things that are difficult to wrap our minds around. I actually tend to prefer tackling complex issues over simple issues, but I realize that both are necessary. And there is also this whole thing where Jesus says that we must become like children to enter the Kingdom (Matthew 18:3).

How do children think?

I think we would be mistaken if we called them simple thinkers. Rather, I think children take complex issues and *make* them simple. They take things that adults wrestle with and make them so unbelievably simple that one cannot help but acknowledge that they were created in the image of God. And while the image of God is in all of us, it is often less distorted in children. Because they have not experienced as much of the brokenness of this present age as we have, they are able to dream more freely of the age to come.

... The kingdom of the world has become the Kingdom of our Lord and of his Messiah, and he will reign for ever and ever.
~ Revelation 11:15

Questions

There will be no questions today, as I have likely already given you enough to think about. Sometimes, we need to ask our own questions, not someone else's. What is stirring in your heart as you read this?

Activation

As we live in the overlap of the ages, we are invited into the reality that it is possible for Heaven to manifest on earth, for Heaven and earth to be the same place. I'm not saying that Heaven and earth literally *are* the same place or that we *always* experience Heaven on earth, I'm just trying to convince you that it is possible.

If it is true that Heaven can come to earth, and if it is true that Heaven and earth can be the same place, where do we see that reality manifested?

Take some time today to really ponder that. We'll discuss it tomorrow.

DAY 19
THE PERSPECTIVE OF HEAVEN

Yesterday, we talked about the overlap of the ages, about living between the *now* and *not yet*, as the Kingdom of God has come, is coming, and will continue to come. But what does that look like today, here and now, in our everyday lives?

The Kingdom of God is not a building or the places that the ministries of the local church touch, though the church is an expression of the Kingdom. Rather, the Kingdom of God is the rule and reign of the government of God that *has come* into the earth (Matthew 3:2) and *is coming* into the earth (Revelation 11:15). *Of the increase of his government and peace there shall be no end ...* ~ *Isaiah 9:7, KJV*

Simply put, the Kingdom of God is the place where God's will is fully expressed and nothing is out of order. It's the place where original design is restored, the place where we fully see who we were created and redeemed to be. The Kingdom of God is Heaven, but it is not limited to Heaven, because God's government has come and is coming into the world just as Jesus came into the world.

The overlap of the ages makes our experience as spiritual beings living in a material world a bit awkward. We see some realities of the Kingdom here on earth, but we also see realities to the contrary. Sometimes, we even see these realities side-by-side, which gives us a glimpse of the stark contrast between this present age and the age to come.

In Romans 12:2, the Apostle Paul urges us, *Do not conform to the pattern of this world, but be transformed by the renewing of your mind.* We often take this to mean that we should stop sinning, read the Bible, and start doing good things. And there is some truth to that, but it is only a partial truth.

When Paul wrote this letter, I don't think his primary concern was his readers not conforming to the pattern of this world. Rather, his primary concern was his readers renewing their minds. To say that Paul's primary concern is the former would place our focus on the wrong thing, in a similar manner to focusing on shallow desires over deeper desires. Paul wants our minds to be renewed, but rather than telling us "renew your mind, or else!" he instead tells us how our minds are *not* renewed: by conforming to the pattern of this world.

What I love about this passage is that Paul does not lay out a simple formula. Instead, he states the desired end, tells us how *not* to get there, and then moves on. There is a portion of this that is left for us to seek out if we desire to put it into action. If our minds are not to conform to the pattern of this world, to this present age, what is the other option? What would be the opposite of that?

The age to come.

In other words, our minds and ways of thinking are transformed when we align them with the reality of the age to come. We abandon ways of thinking related to this present age, so that we can see reality from the perspective of Heaven, and thus pull it into the earthly realm. This idea is illustrated in James 3:15-17, where James talks about two types of wisdom: heavenly wisdom and earthly wisdom; wisdom from the age to come and wisdom from this present age.

As I asked yesterday, where do we see the reality of Heaven and earth occupying the same place manifested? We cannot say "earth," because that is too broad of a term, and we certainly do not see the reality of Heaven fully manifested on earth at present. I don't think we can even say "in the church," because that is also far too broad, and I've been to plenty of churches where the reality of Heaven is not expressed at all (and some churches where even the opposite is expressed).

For the record, I'm *not* referring to styles of worship or the exercise of spiritual gifts. You can have a very reverent and orderly service that brings Heaven to earth, and you can also have a very expressive and "spirit-filled" service that brings Hell to earth. It's more about *what* you're releasing into the atmosphere than the *way* in which you release it.

There's a clue there; did you catch it?

It's about <u>what</u> you release into the atmosphere.

The Kingdom of God is all around us, but we don't always experience it. The Kingdom is not something that can be fully contained, but it is something that we can *contain*, which means it is something that we can *release*. In a similar manner, the kingdom of darkness (the ruling force behind this present age) is something that can be contained and released as well.

There is a way of interpreting Luke 17:21 that says the Kingdom is within us, and so all we must do is look inside of ourselves to find it. This is mostly false, but there is a shard of truth in it. To say that the Kingdom is *within* us is to imply that the Kingdom is *from* us. But the Kingdom is not from us, it is from God. We cannot create it within ourselves, but we can receive it as a gift. While some versions of the Bible translate Luke 17:21 to say that the Kingdom is inside of us, others translate it more correctly as *the Kingdom of God is in your midst.* And for the shard of truth, when we receive the Kingdom as a gift, we can contain it within ourselves and release it wherever we go. The Kingdom does not originate within the hearts of men, but it can dwell in the good heart that Jesus gave you when He redeemed you.

Paul prayed that the King would live in our hearts through faith (Ephesians 3:17), and when the King comes, He brings the Kingdom with Him. He also tells us that our bodies are temples where the Holy Spirit lives (1 Corinthians 6:19). We can see that the King can live inside of us and we can release the Kingdom to the world around us, but we must just remember that this ability is not *from* us. (2 Corinthians 4:7).

The Kingdom of God is the rule and reign of the government of God, both on earth *now* and coming to earth *not yet.* When we renew our minds, we seek to live as citizens of the Kingdom first and citizens of earth second. This means that we import the ways of the Kingdom from eternity into time and space and live as if they were *already true.* When we live as though this reality is already true on earth, just as it is in Heaven, we release the Kingdom into the world around us and become the place where Heaven and earth are the same place.

We are being drawn toward a day where Heaven and earth are the same place, which will fully occur when Jesus returns. But isn't it interesting that we are told to not just *wait* for that day, but to begin to *live* as if it were already true?

So, my friend, breathe in His life, breathe in His love; exhale the ways of this present age, the ways of the bad father. Seek to live under the rule and reign of the government of God, to learn the ways of the Kingdom. Let the reality of the age to come renew your mind, so that you may see and think and feel from the perspective of Heaven. And as you gather within the walls of the church, around the dinner table, or at Walmart, remember that the King lives inside of you, and you can release His life wherever you go. You can introduce Him to others and invite them to experience the Kingdom, because it is right here in our midst.

Faith gives us a glimpse of God's vision of tomorrow, enabling us to live now in light of what is not yet. ~ Alan Smith

Questions

1) How has today's discussion changed the way you previously thought about renewing your mind?

2) Do you feel worthy to have the King live in your heart through faith? Why or why not?

3) What would it look like to bring the Kingdom to Walmart, without being obnoxious about it?

Activation

This afternoon, I went for a walk in my neighborhood. At one point, I saw a well-dressed couple getting out of their car in front of a construction site. He was in business attire; she was in a dress that was nearly floor-length. As I passed by, I watched as they carefully made their way through the yard, which was nothing more than a pile of dirt and rocks. As they approached the concrete slab that would soon become their front porch, I watched as the man climbed up first before reaching down to help his wife up onto the slab. They then entered the house, which was little more than an exterior shell and wood-framed interior walls.

As I continued on my way, I began to think of the Parable of the Wedding Banquet that Jesus told in Matthew 22. In this parable, a king prepared a wedding banquet for his son, but none of the guests who had been invited bothered to show up. So the king sent his servants out in an attempt to convince them to come, but they refused. When the servants returned alone, the king was frustrated.

"The wedding banquet is ready!" he told them.

"What should we do?" they asked. "No one that was invited has come."

"Go to the streets and invite anyone you can find. If they will come, let them come."

So the servants went out into the streets and gathered all the people they could find, the bad as well as the good, and the wedding hall was filled with guests. ~ Matthew 22:10

My favorite part of this verse is that the bad came along with the good. They weren't invited because they had done anything to deserve it, but simply because they put on their wedding clothes and came.

When I thought about that couple walking into their future home—which was still a mess at that point—I couldn't help but think to myself, *their home is far from finished, but they've got their wedding clothes on.*

This is a lot like our lives here on earth. We can see a form of the Kingdom around us, but it still feels as though we are living in a construction site; what is already true in Heaven is far from becoming fully true on earth. Yet, we still put on our wedding clothes and trudge through the mess to imagine the possibilities that will soon no longer be dreams.

When we begin to look at our lives on earth from the perspective of Heaven, we wake up each morning and put on our wedding clothes, even though we know we still have to enter a war zone for now. We don't let the brokenness of the world keep us from clothing ourselves in the reality of the age to come. We are dressed for the wedding, and we can invite others to the wedding as well. We can even bring a preview of the wedding into this present reality, because we are the place where Heaven and earth are the same place.

DAY 20
COMMUNITY

Last fall, I was visiting my friends, Mark and Jessica Royalty, in South Dakota, when an unexpected blizzard dumped two feet of snow on their city. Our side of the street lost power for 72 hours, but the other side of the street managed to retain power throughout the storm. Fortunately, Mark and Jessica were close with many of their neighbors on the other side of the street, so we would trudge back and forth through waist-deep snow drifts for meals, games, and just hanging out at the houses that had power.

When Sunday morning rolled around, much of the city was still snowed in, so we made our way back across the street for church at Bryan and Laura's house. Bryan, a local pastor, affectionately referred to this gathering as "Church in the Hood."

Several more neighbors trickled in, until there were five or six families packed into Bryan and Laura's living room. We sang a few songs, and then Bryan got up and spoke for a bit. What I loved most about his talk was that he did not leverage it as an opportunity to show off his preaching skills for his neighbors, who normally attended different churches when they could get their cars out of their driveways. Instead, Bryan talked about the value of community, using Ephesians 2:10 as his text.

For we are His workmanship, created in Christ Jesus for good works, which God prepared beforehand so that we would walk in them. ~ Ephesians 2:10, NASB

I had heard this verse preached several times, but never the way that Bryan talked about it. I had heard it said that the Greek word for *workmanship* meant *one-of-a-kind masterpiece,* meaning that I, personally, am God's one-of-a-kind-masterpiece, created for good works. This verse both inspired and shamed me at the same time. It's wonderful to know that I'm God's masterpiece, but I always felt like I wasn't very good at the *good works* part. I would get involved with whatever outreach events my church was doing, but I couldn't seem to find my own good works to walk in. The way that Bryan talked about this verse was quite liberating for me. He told us that *workmanship* carried a corporate context over an individual one, which means that, collectively, we are *God's masterpiece, God's rhyme, God's poem.* Bryan said that this particular group of believers gathered on this particular block on the west side of Rapid City were God's poem within their community, and that each individual person composed a different line of that poem. Within minutes, he had completely wrecked my understanding of this verse.

When you look at the context of Ephesians 2—as well as the greater book of Ephesians—you will see that the whole thing is corporate. While there are a few things here and there that address the individual, Paul is primarily conveying his message to the community as a whole. For example, verses 8-9 of Ephesians 2 speak of God's work in individual hearts, but then verse 10 moves back to a corporate perspective when it says _we are His workmanship_.

This new way of seeing Scripture has relieved me of the pressure I previously felt to go out and do something great for God on my own, because I know that I am part of a larger community, and becoming God's workmanship is something we do collectively when we all come together. What I mean by that is, I no longer feel the burden to change my community by myself, because I have realized that it's not about me, myself, and I walking in good works, but my corporate community of believers from different churches and backgrounds walking in good works together. This means that we _all_ share the burden for reaching our community; no one person has to carry it alone. This is good news, because I am becoming increasingly aware that, while I can do good works on my own at some level, the impact is so much greater when we all come together.

When you enter the Kingdom of God, you enter God's family. When you join a local church, you become a part of a family within a family. Both the local church expression and the larger family of God are the *workmanship, the masterpiece, the poem* that we've been talking about. (Think of the local expression as a poem, and the larger family as a book of poems.)

Being a part of a local expression is important, because otherwise, you're not part of a defined poem within the book of poems. Perhaps there is a separate poem at the end for those who are not part of a defined poem, but that poem doesn't make much sense, because it's composed of people who are moving in different directions and whose paths have yet to intersect. While God's family is the larger Body of Christ, you can never really say you are a functioning part of the family until you are a part of a family within the family. Sure, you're *in* the family, but unless you take part in a local expression, it's no different than being related to people that you only visit once or twice a year.

I said all of that to say this: Because God's workmanship is not you or me on our own, there is an aspect of our identity that can only be found in community. I am not saying you need to join a specific type of church or that you need to meet in a traditional building for a traditional service. What I am saying is that you need to be a part of some sort of expression of the Kingdom, some sort of poem. The details don't matter; you just need to find an ongoing expression and become a line in the poem that is being written. This will not happen if you go from expression to expression each week for the rest of your life. However, like the folks in Rapid City, if you are in the larger family, I suppose you could be a part of the poem in your neighborhood, even if you don't attend a service on the weekends. This would, however, require you to know your neighbors, because you don't become a part of the poem simply by existing and believing in Jesus. That gets you in the family, yes, but you can be in the family and not be taking part in writing the poem.

The purpose of this discussion is not to diminish the greatness that God has put inside of you; that would undo everything this devotional has been trying to accomplish. God has made you unique and awesome, but you are not the total package. You are not His full workmanship, just another line of the poem. So, whether you possess many talents or few, whether you are outgoing or reclusive, whether you are alive and awake or broken and battered;

come. Come and partake in the portion of your identity that can only be found in community.

Church is a place where God is forming a family out of strangers.
~ Glenn Packiam

Questions

1) How has today's discussion shifted your understanding of church from individual-focused to community-focused?

2) Are you currently an active member of a local church? Why or why not?

3) If you're not part of a local church, what's stopping you? If you're not actively involved in the church you currently attend, what's holding you back?

Activation

You know what I love about the local church? There are so many unique expressions. This diversity is often the point of divisions and arguments, but I believe it is something that we should celebrate. Whether you go to a traditional church that meets in a historic building with wood pews and stained glass windows, a modern church that meets in a renovated grocery store, or a house church that meets in a neighborhood, each church is a unique expression of the Kingdom of God; each church is a one-of-a-kind masterpiece. The Kingdom of God is not your church or my church; the Kingdom of God is when we all come together. But in the context of weekly expressions, it's okay that we meet in different places and have different styles. Often, it's not that one church is right and another is wrong, but each church is a different expression of God. Because God is so much bigger than our minds could ever comprehend, it's possible for two churches to be polar opposites, yet still bear the image of the same God. We don't all look the same, and that's okay.

If you're not currently a part of a weekly expression, I encourage you to find one and begin attending. And if you are a part of a weekly expression, but you vacate the building the moment the service ends, I encourage you to find a way to become more involved. Church is not about putting your butt in a seat for an hour, but being part of a family, and it's hard to get to know your family when you never talk to them. I realize that you may have drawn back from the church due to past hurts. I have too—several times. I have been hurt by the church. But I have also been healed by the church.

DAY 21
SHELTER FROM THE STORM

Over the past twenty days, we've discussed how to make sense of our lives, heal old wounds, and become who God created and redeemed us to be. But where do we go from here? What do we do with new wounds as they happen? What will our moment-to-moment response to life in a world at war be?

Hopefully, I've given you lots of helpful tools, but really, all you need to know is you live in a world at war, there are two fathers fighting for your heart, and you can connect with your True Father in the midst of it all. Everything else is secondary to that.

Because the war never stops waging around us, it is essential that we protect our hearts. This doesn't mean that we disengage, but rather, that we engage properly. To engage properly in a world at war doesn't mean that we put our hearts out there to get pummeled, but that we know how to put our hearts on the line, to risk, at appropriate times. In order to stay engaged, it is essential that we have a safe place to retreat to—a shelter from the storm. This is not a shelter that we hide out in so that we can remain disengaged, but a shelter that we can retreat to when our hearts are getting beat down, in order to find rest, healing, and strength before we put ourselves back out there. If we believe that staying engaged looks like never seeking shelter from the storm, we'll eventually find our hearts crumbling. When this happens, we'll retreat to the shelter—not to find rest, but to hide.

The Lord is my rock, my fortress and my deliverer; my God is my rock, in whom I take refuge, my shield and the horn of my salvation, my stronghold. ~ *Psalm 18:2*

Your True Father is your place of refuge, your shelter from the storm. When you're caught in the fallout of a world at war, it's crucial that you keep your heart open and connected to God. It's in those moments, when you experience hurt, pain, or rejection, that the bad father will offer you answers as to why those things have happened. His goal is to suppress your heart and shut off your connection with your True Father, mostly by getting you to believe a false interpretation of the events of your life, otherwise known as lies.

Jesus told us that we would have trouble in this world (John 16:33), but that doesn't mean that our lives have to spin out of control. Life is generally 10% what happens to us and 90% how we respond to it. This is why it's so important to properly process new wounds as they happen, because the bad father wants those wounds to go unhealed and grow larger, until they cover and bury your heart, cutting off the source of life that flows between you and your True Father.

As the church, we serve a God who is a shelter from the storm, which means that we should be shelters from the storm as well. There are people in our communities who have been battered and torn apart by life, and they don't always know how to find their way home to God. But they likely pass by churches every day, houses where God is forming families out of strangers. Do they know that these houses are shelters from the storm, or do they view them primarily as houses of exclusivity and judgment?

I was at a Bible club in a local high school last week when I struck up a conversation with a student who showed little emotion. I kept prying for some sort of response out of him, but he would barely look at me. After the club was over, I was talking to the mother of the girl who leads the club, and she told me that the student I had been talking to earlier is an atheist with a rough home life. Still, he's been coming to the Bible club week after week. He sits there, in the back row, unengaged. A mere spectator, he doesn't join in with the conversation, or even crack a smile, but he's there—week after week. Perhaps he has realized that the Bible club is a shelter from the storm.

It's not a church, but it *is* a place where the people of God meet on a weekly basis as they seek to bring an awareness of who He is to their campus. It's a safe place, a place where people can connect to God and His people. Because a shelter from the storm is not just about a building, it's about us coming to look like our True Father, who is a shelter from the storm for all who desire to take refuge.

The work of our salvation takes place in the midst of a world that continues to shout, scream, and overwhelm us with its claims and promises. ~ Henri Nouwen

Questions

1) Who or what do you run to when your life feels like it's falling apart?

2) Are you a shelter from the storm to people around you? Do people know they can trust you?

3) Is your church a place that the people in the community would consider a shelter from the storm? Why or why not? What can you do to improve this?

Activation

Yesterday, I was helping out with a community outreach in a nearby city. After an assembly at the local high school, I invited a student to come back to a service that night at a local church, where we would preach the Gospel.

"No, thanks," he politely declined. "I'm not really a religious person."

"That's okay," I told him. "You're still welcome to come."

"I know," he said. "That's the great thing about church—everyone's welcome."

He walked away, leaving me stunned.

I've never met anyone who had such a positive view of church, but still didn't want to have anything to do with it. Most of the people who fall into that category have been hurt terribly by the church—or someone who represented God—while they were trying to seek shelter from the storm. But this guy ... this guy got it. He knew that the church where we were holding the outreach was a shelter from the storm, a place he could run to if life ever got the best of him.

I wonder if my church has that reputation? I wonder if we are known as a shelter from the storm—one of many—in our community? I wonder if people, regardless of how they feel about Jesus, would miss us if we shut our doors tomorrow, because they know that we make the community a better place.

Those who want nothing to do with Jesus live in the same war zone that we do; they just don't know what it's like to recover their hearts and re-connect to their True Father. But storms will come, and when they do, they will seek shelter. Before they turn to the local church, they will likely turn to drugs and alcohol, sex and money, or power and control. This is why we need to have a reputation for loving and accepting people who deal with these things, so that empty people who have tried everything else can come into our buildings and lives and find shelter from the storm. Perhaps they will even discover who they were created and redeemed to be in the process. How beautiful would that be, for people to come seeking relief from pain and leave fully restored?

What can you do to help make your church a more accessible shelter from the storm? And what can you do to make *yourself* a more accessible shelter from the storm? Not everyone will walk through the doors of a church, but if they know that you are a safe place they may open up to you instead. And when they do, you can connect them with their True Father, because you know Him and are full of His love.

Available soon from Battle Ground Creative

To connect with Jared, please visit www.jaredstump.com or follow him on Twitter: @jaredstump

Battle Ground Creative is a faith-based publishing company with an emphasis on helping first-time authors find their voice. Named after an obscure city in Washington State, we currently operate offices in Dallas, Texas and Harrisburg, Pennsylvania. For a complete title list and bulk order information, please visit www.battlegroundcreative.com

20804093R00077

Made in the USA
Middletown, DE
09 June 2015